PERSECUTED

Elwood McQuaid

HARVEST HOUSE™PUBLISHERS

EUGENE, OREGON

Cover by Left Coast Design, Portland, Oregon

PERSECUTED
Copyright © 2003 by Elwood McQuaid
Published by Harvest House Publishers
Eugene, Oregon 97402

Library of Congress Cataloging-in-Publication Data
McQuaid, Elwood.
        Persecuted / Elwood McQuaid.
                p. cm.
Includes bibliographical references.
        ISBN 0-7369-0162-0 (pbk.)
        1. Persecution—History—20th century.   2. Christian martyrs—
History—20th century. 3. Evangelical Church—History—20th century.
        4. Church history—20th century.   I. Title.
        BR1601.3 .M36 2002
        272'.9—dc21   2002011819

Printed in the United States of America.

        03   04   05   06   07   08   09   10   / DP-CF /   10   9   8   7   6   5   4   3   2   1

CONTENTS

Marked for Extinction

THE PASTOR LAY ON THE FLOOR of the church in a pool of blood. Scattered before his lifeless body were his broken glasses, Bible, and a blood-spattered hymnal. In a corner of the church auditorium lay the bodies of three female parishioners. One woman's facial expression was frozen into a look of total unbelief. It was almost as if her pallid face was saying that this horror could not be happening to them. Not in this place—not in a Christian church, the house of God. But it had. The massacre took place in Pakistan. It occurred as American forces were hammering the Taliban and Osama bin Laden's al Qaeda in neighboring Afghanistan. During the worship service three Muslim terrorists burst into the church shouting *Allah Ahkbar* (God is great), opened fire, and emptied 500 rounds of ammunition into the assembled congregants. By the time the terrorists fled the scene, 15 worshipers were dead and many others wounded.

A few years ago, such a catastrophe would have sent shock waves through the Christian community worldwide. Articles and books would have been written, prayer vigils held, memorial services conducted, and sermons given about dying for the faith and the distinction of wearing a martyr's crown. None of these things occurred. The tragedy was not lamented as a catastrophe; it was hardly even acknowledged as an incident.

It is being commonly reported that more Christians have died for their faith in this generation than at any other time in the 2000-year history of the Christian church. If that is true, why does a seemingly impenetrable shroud of silence exist? One can understand why politically correct secularists choose not to pay attention. For one thing, it doesn't align with their agenda. For another, they aren't interested. The deaths of Christians falls too far down on the scale of their priorities. Christians, and their faith, are judged irrelevant to matters worth paying serious attention to. So we should not be greatly surprised at the general lack of concern. But what can be said about Christians themselves and evangelicals in particular? Why this virtual silence in our pulpits, publications, and broadcast media?

As is most frequently the case, it is not difficult for commentators and writers to raise such questions. However, identifying the problems and offering some explanation as to why they exist is quite another matter. Regarding the question of the persecution of Christians, one gropes for explanations, and more importantly, asks if there are adequate answers as to what should be done. The answer to both those queries is yes. And surprising as it may seem, getting to the heart of why things are like they are is not actually a difficult task. For one reason, the subject has been adequately researched and publicized. The problem is that with only rare exceptions have these information sources been adequately exposed and related to the current situation for Christians. This is especially true as they contribute insights into the worldwide campaign of terror being waged against believers.

Do evangelical Christians need a proverbial wake-up call? The question is, of course, rhetorical. Some will respond by assuring us that the call has already come, and the response has been overwhelming. The bell, they will contend, rang on the morning of September 11, 2001 amid fiery explosions and death falling from the sky in New York, Washington, and a field in Pennsylvania. In one sense the observation is correct. Americans suddenly found themselves in a world that was heretofore foreign to their experience.

Humorist Art Buchwald wrote, "On September 11, 2001, I lost my center. That is, the world as I knew it crashed in on me, as it did everyone else in America.

"Before that day, I had dreams for my children and grand-children. I felt safe....

"I tried to go about my business as I did before, but it wasn't the same and it never would be.

"I tried to make plans for the future, but my heart wasn't in it....

"For the first time I knew there was somebody out there who wanted to kill me.

"It was not a movie."[1]

Millions of Americans shared Mr. Buchwald's despair as a profound feeling of being traumatized by a wave of terror that didn't seem to make sense began to take hold. But in the immediate wake of the attack, Americans, in the grips of the enormity of the threat, came to the side of President Bush in a national surge of patriotism and unity. Throughout the country flags blossomed from every conceivable vantage point. Quite frankly, the resounding outburst of national loyalty was the manifestation of a phenomenon many had questioned could ever be evoked in our citizens again. But now Americans knew that there was a world out there hostile to our democracy, our freedom, our toleration, and our very existence as a country. It was, indeed, a cruel awakening.

But how deeply did the awakening run? Unfortunately, it didn't translate into a national awareness that the horrific American tragedy was somehow related to the experience of thousands of Christians who are being slain in many parts of the world by the same forces that slammed those commandeered jetliners into American institutions. Of course, the majority of the innocent victims of the current wave of global terrorism against Christians are not Americans, but they were being marked for extinction for the same reasons as the unfortunate thousands in the World Trade Center and Pentagon.

And perhaps there is an important corollary to the inability to make this connection. Amid all of the admirable rallying to a sense of patriotism, country, and duty there was little evidence of a wave of true turning to God. Yes, there were memorial services and other religious observances, but the spiritual aspects seemed, while certainly not for everyone, for the majority superficial at best. There was no evidence of a massive turn toward national and personal repentance. It is perhaps in this arena that the War on Terror has its weakest element.

Any analysis of how and why such weakness has become a part of the fiber of much of evangelicalism must begin with a look back. A decade ago an American administration rode into power glibly admonishing us in song to not stop thinking about tomorrow. The aura over their bridge to a brighter future was to scrap the past and move into the New World Order enunciated by their political predecessors. Theirs would be a "Global Village"—but a village with a very different cast from what we remember as traditional America. And before we are tempted to heap scorn on this cast of political and social revolutionaries, we will do well to remember that they were but products of the culture in which they were reared.

America, and much of the West, has undergone a major cultural revolution. This social, political, and cultural convulsion did not begin at the top and work its way down; it rose up from the grassroots, from the foundation upon which the nation rested for more than two centuries. It was a slow spiritual degeneration that eventually began to pollute the life source of the country. We Americans, because of our tenacious grasp on the quite properly cherished concept of the separation of church and state, miss a fundamental fact of life that is operative in much of the rest of the world. Here secularists have come to believe that politics and social libertarianism drive the system, and that the influences of religion, particularly Christianity, and even more particularly evangelical Christianity, must be purged from our national life and shunted off into purely religious institutions. This kind of thinking has resulted in a systematic repudiation of our Judeo-Christian underpinnings, creating an increasingly adversarial environment. To our detriment, this hostile approach has placed the very future of the most successful governmental system in the history of the world in serious jeopardy.

Much of the rest of the world does not see life or operate governments in the way we in the Western democracies do. In their world it is religion that drives politics, social mores, military concepts, judicial systems, and virtually every other aspect of life. An obvious example is found in Islamic countries. For them, the ideal is for Islamic law *(Shari'a)* to be instituted as the law of the land. There is no separation of religion and the state. Religion *is* the state. Pluralism is a concept that is unknown and is not welcomed in the Islamic world. For this reason democracies have great difficulty in negotiations with Islamists on issues such as human rights, free elections, or territorial concepts. Western leaders insist on the self-imposed delusion that we basically, as human beings, think and reason in the same ways. In some essential areas, however, we do not. The delusion bears serious consequences.

It may be of little comfort, but Americans have not fallen into the current cultural quagmire alone. Our British cousins have gone before us blazing a dubious path that we could possibly have avoided if only we had allowed history to teach us. But, as is often axiomatically lamented, we did not. We have neglected to recognize that the same irrational secular forces have for decades been running across the Atlantic that are flowing here in the United States.

Therefore, it is well for us to look back at the way it once was. Not in a maudlin, self-pitying exercise in how to throw up our hands in collective despair, but rather with the understanding that a look back is actually a look inside ourselves. Because we are, whether we acknowledge it or not, in many respects inevitably products of the past. Thus, it will do well for us to look inside and see how much of what was planted is still there. I think you may be surprised at what you find. Perhaps it will be a discovery that will lead to a reawakening and consequent revitalization of your life and a renewed commitment to our Lord's calling for your life.

This book is offered in an attempt to examine the way it once was in American life, then move on to examine what went wrong. How did this great Republic, with all of its promise, get derailed? It is absolutely essential for every citizen of this country, particularly Christians, to understand exactly what has befallen us. And in a larger sense, we are compelled to examine the clash of cultures, religious and secular, that is taking place in our lifetime. It is, in an almost depressing way, a fight to the finish. In actuality, it is an ancient conflict reborn. On the one hand, pagan philosophies and lifestyles have emerged that defy and challenge the Judeo-Christian way of life that has been the norm in America since the founding of the Republic. On the other hand, radical Islamic expansionism is something barely understood or reluctantly acknowledged. And whatever quarter these threats approach us from, millions of affluent, self-satisfied citizens are not about to be moved off dead center. The status quo is the stuff of life for our society. Be that as it may, ominous forces are on the attack. They make no secret of their determination to destroy the way of life we have come to accept as both comfortable and normal. Can our way of life be disrupted or even destroyed? Most of us think probably not. Our adversaries think differently. And while we may choose not to entertain such ominous thoughts, what is happening to our Christian brothers and sisters in other parts of the world can indeed happen to us.

As Art Buchwald postulated, someone out there wants to kill you and me.

A major problem has, without question, been our insulation by affluence. Our unparalleled economic enrichment has come to us as both a blessing and a curse. It was the former aid to President Nixon, Charles Colson, who once said that this generation of Christians has been "co-opted by the culture." Colson was correct. While we may protest this being the case, the facts are irrefutable.

And while most in the Western world choose to dabble in contemporary irrelevance, the line of martyrs continues to grow ever longer. A news agency reported that in one year alone at least 160,000 Christians were slaughtered for their faith in Christ. Have we been moved? Are we outraged? Are we anguished? Do we weep aloud for those brethren forced to suffer and cry in silence? Certainly not in ways that anyone has noticed to any significant degree.

Today, there is the inescapable reality that evangelical Christians are rapidly becoming misfits in the new global society. Although we have never experienced any serious degree of persecution for our faith, the phenomenon is nothing new. The suffering church has been more often the norm than the exception for the past two millennia. And if we are not inclined to pay attention now, we will certainly be forced to the issue in the not-too-distant future. Will we awaken then?

Time will tell. But I am personally compelled to believe that if and when persecution comes to our doorsteps, true believers will stand true. As in the past, pretenders will be purged, but the true church, albeit under severe suffering, will be victorious.

Verification of my confidence will emerge as you read the testimonies of martyrs, mutilated believers, and their family members who have, humanly speaking, suffered irreparable loss, yet experienced in the fullest possible way the sheer majesty of the total triumph of Christ. In spite of indescribable horrors they have been subjected to, their faith has endured and emerged in the form of courage, determination, steadfastness, and a deep and abiding love and devotion to their Savior.

So, in simple terms, although this book is one of information, analysis, and warnings, it is actually an exercise in hope, encouragement, and preparation for whatever the future may hold.

Ultimately, it is offered in the spirit articulated by the apostle Paul:

> Wherefore, take unto you the whole armor of God, that you may be able to withstand in the evil day, and having done all to stand (Ephesians 6:13).

CHAPTER ONE

Rescue those being led away to death;
hold back those staggering toward slaughter.
If you say, "But we knew nothing about this,"
Does not he who weighs the heart perceive it?
Does not he who guards your life know it? Will
He not repay each person according to what
he has done?

PROVERBS 24:11-12 (NIV)

An Age of Innocence

The nation we live in today is more violent and vulgar, coarse and cynical, rude and remorseless, deviant and depressed, than the one we once inhabited. A popular culture that is brutal, gruesome, and enamored with death robs many children of their innocence. People kill other people, and themselves, more easily. Men and women abandon each other, and their children, more readily. Marriage and the American family are weaker, more unstable, less normative.[2]

THIS IN-YOUR-FACE EVALUATION BY William J. Bennett of what the American culture has evolved into will all at once cause "liberated" social progressives to recoil in anger and others to nod in sober, reflective agreement. The fact is that this is precisely where the line is drawn between what once was considered the cherished birthright of every American generation, and the social wrecking crews determined to build their version of a brave new world on the ashes of time-tested American traditions.

For me, the issues at hand were never more clearly expressed than in the words of a brash young college student during the campus riots of the 1960s. During those tumultuous days roving gangs of America's future leaders were holding college presidents hostage, draping themselves all over the floors of university administration buildings, and exchanging pep-rally bonfires for incinerating campus buildings.

On one such occasion a reporter approached a student with a question about what was going on.

"We're burning this building to the ground."

"Why?" queried the reporter.

"It's a protest against the establishment," said the student.

"But if this is a symbol of destroying the establishment, what do you intend to build in its place?"

"I have no idea," replied the young revolutionary. "We're just going to burn it down and see what comes up out of the ashes."

Some 40 years later, Mr. Bennett has described what has come "up out of the ashes."

The Bliss of the Past

A brief excursion back into the mid-1930s will expose a slice of the innocence now, unfortunately, lost to us and to our children. A typical day in an elementary school in the Midwest began with a prayer, a pledge of allegiance to the flag, and the singing of a patriotic song. All this was done under the solemn gaze of Abraham Lincoln and the Father of our country, George Washington. Respect for these men and other founding fathers was drilled into youngsters from the first day we stepped into a kindergarten classroom. This kind of instruction was accompanied by a heavy dose of respect for authority in general. Teachers, officers of the law, clergymen, parents, the rules, and the elderly were viewed with a sense of respect closely akin to a kind of reverential awe.

The major offenses in American schools in those days were such grave transgressions as chewing gum in class or conversing at any time class was in session. Running in the halls and hurling much maligned "spit balls" were major offenses that were apt to land perpetrators in the principal's office—a place of dark mysteries and fearsome myths. And of course, at this time the use of the paddle in schools was still in vogue, often reinforced by another paddling at the end of the day if father got wind of the incident. In the current environment, paddle-wielding educators would be carted off in cuffs and charged with inflicting cruel and inhuman punishment upon defenseless children.

After mentioning in a message years ago that my father and I had taken more trips to the woodshed than I care to remember, a psychologist who had attended the meeting approached me.

"I find it quite troubling," he said, "that you would see any humor in telling a public audience that you were an abused child."

"Well," I responded, "If I was an abused child, then every kid growing up in my neighborhood was abused. Every household implemented discipline in those days."

What might shock some contemporary social wardens is that I know of no child in my class or small town who grew up to be serial killers, rapists, wife beaters, child abusers, or murderers of parents while they slept. Insofar as I am aware, they all grew up as pretty decent citizens, law-abiding people, and responsible members of society. Child advocacy in those days wasn't the province of children who charged beleagured educators with inflicting insufferable restrictions on their inherent rights of self-expression. Authorities were not put on trial by miscreant and overindulged youngsters. The system was geared toward learning, discipline, and inculcating respect for authority at all levels.

And this standard went beyond the confines of local school classroom settings. Actually, what went on within the classrooms was only a reflection of the culture that dominated that now lost and scorned era of innocence.

I was reared in a small community in Michigan where orthodox Christianity was far from the order of the day. Beer gardens outnumbered the churches, and to say that ours was a Christian community was a stretch that few would have dared make. That being said, the environment in which our lives moved was immersed in Judeo-Christian morals, ethics, and values. Everyone understood how wrong it was to be a thief, a liar, or a morally corrupt person. We all knew what it meant to be on the wrong side of the law. These were never questions open to debate. We knew what it meant to be a "bad guy." We also understood with pristine clarity what it meant to be a good person. There was never any blurring of the lines between right and wrong.

Looking back, through the prism of the current cultural mores, I can say that ours was indeed an era of innocence in America.

How and why did our society change—in a single generation—to become marked by rampant cynicism—the kind that would breed the callous indifference we now suffer to the detriment of our society and fellow citizens?

In some respects, it is an enigma. The transition and the changes that came with it have been pondered, written of, dissected, and debated. But when all is said and done, a new reality came on the scene—one that would dramatically change how our society felt about other human beings. And, as an important component, how the value of life, especially that of evangelical Christians, was being diminished.

A World That Lost Its Heart

For 14 years a veteran missionary to India, 58-year-old Graham Staines, had ministered to the lepers in the remote village of Manoharpur. On one of his annual visits he chose to take his sons Philip, ten years of age, and Timothy, six years old, along on the journey. For Philip and Timothy the trip was an exciting adventure. The village had no electricity, running water, or other modern amenities. Adding to the excitement was the fact that the three of them would have to spend the night in Graham's Jeep station wagon before going to minister in the village the next day.

As they walked to the vehicle on January 23, 1999, torches in their hands, they chatted about the adventures of the day. Spending time among these simple people who had shown such love and respect to them and their father had simply been a wonderful experience for the boys. Once inside their crowded quarters they settled down for what they thought would be a refreshing night of rest. As was their usual practice, the three prayed for mother Gladys, the family left behind, the inmates of the leprosy home, the nation, and Christians all over the world.

While they were praying and settling in for the night, a mob of Hindu militants approached the village. At approximately 12:20 A.M. they came upon the Staines's station wagon and began slashing the tires, breaking out the windows, and thrusting spears at the missionary and his terrified boys. In the attack, Graham and his sons were beaten mercilessly. Finally, the leader of the mob placed straw under the vehicle and set it on fire. As the flames intensified, the Staines were prevented from escaping by the fanatics bent on seeing them burned alive. Graham held the two boys close to him as the inferno engulfed the station wagon. Screaming villagers were trapped in their houses as Graham and his sons were incinerated; anyone who tried to help put out the flames was driven away.

Dr. Subhankar Ghosh, a close friend of the Staines, recalls the tragic events.

> We had dinner with the Staines around 9 P.M. and they went to sleep in the Willys station wagon, parked near the church around 9:45 P.M. I was sleeping along with Mr. Gilbert Venz, an overseas friend of the Staines, in one of the huts, hardly 200 meters from the chapel. By midnight, we were woken up by some strange shouts and screams, and I peeped through the side window. I couldn't believe what I saw. I heard shouts, screams, beatings, banging of doors. There were about 50–60 people with torches in their hands....Soon they started smashing the windows of the jeep with bars and sticks. The frenzied crowd blocked Graham from escaping with his children. They were brutally beaten. Then suddenly I saw the jeep in flames. I knew my dear friends would be turned into ashes.[3]

When wife Gladys and her 13-year-old daughter were told of the murders, they reacted in a way that astounded many of the people around them. Daughter Esther remarked, "I am proud that my father was considered worthy to die for God."

Standing by the bodies of her husband and two sons, Gladys Staines said, "It is the sovereign will of God that my husband should die."

Someone asked how a teenage girl could know such things about God. "She speaks as though God was her personal friend with whom she has a daily talk!"

"And how can a widow, on hearing such ghastly news, speak so calmly and think of God and His will during these terrible moments?! A blind faith that induces its gullible followers to embrace death for a utopian cause? Or is Jesus Christ really worth dying for?"[4]

With Graham Staines and his sons, Philip and Timothy, safely with the Lord at home in glory, Esther and Gladys Staines knew beyond any shadow of a doubt that Jesus Christ is really worth dying for. But far away in the West, affluent Christians went about their business, unaware that anything was amiss with their brothers in far-off India. In the days to come, the impact of this terrible tragedy would cause hardly more than a ripple.

Why? What had changed since the worldwide outcry in 1956 when members of the primitive Auca tribe martyred five young missionaries on the banks of the Curaray River in the jungles of Ecuador?

Perhaps you're familiar with that story. Jim Elliot, then husband of Elisabeth Elliot, and four of his missionary friends were killed by the Auca Indians. Christians were mobilized to pray for the Aucas and the bereaved families. Evangelicals were in shock and the names of the five young missionaries were memorialized in sermons, books, and songs. What's more, the five missionaries' attitude toward martyrdom—much like that of Graham Staines's—was summed up in what have become legendary words written by one of the slain men himself. Jim Elliot, as a college student in 1949: "He is no fool who gives what he cannot keep to gain what he cannot lose."[5]

But the martyrdom of those courageous men seems to have taken place a very long time ago, in a world far removed from our own. We've now moved on to other things—but not better things.

According to figures compiled by former U.S. Secretary of Education William J. Bennett, America is headed in a vastly new and different direction.

Since 1960, our population has increased by 48%. But since 1960, even taking into account recent improvements, we have seen a 467 percent increase in violent crime; a 463 percent increase in the numbers of state and federal prisoners; a 461 percent increase in out-of-wedlock births; more than a 200 percent increase in the percentage of children living in single-parent homes; more than a doubling in the teenage suicide rate; a more than 150 percent increase in the number of Americans receiving welfare payments; an almost tenfold increase in the number of [out of wedlock] cohabiting couples; a doubling of the divorce rate; and a drop of almost 60 points on SAT scores. Since 1973, there have been more than 35 million abortions, increasing from 744,060 in 1973 to 1,365,700 in 1996....Even during a time of record prosperity many Americans believe something has gone wrong at the core.[6]

Something has indeed gone wrong at the core—very wrong. And at a juncture in history where many are confused about what has hit us and are frantically trying to repair the system, they are looking for answers in the wrong places and attempting to apply solutions that will make little or no appreciable difference. In fact, much of the tinkering by politicians and social planners will do more harm than good.

The Core Problem

The reason for this pervasive inadequacy is that the core problem is spiritual, and virtually none of the self-appointed "fixers" of this generation are equipped to confront our problems on a spiritual plane. Quite the opposite. They write off biblical, spiritual, and moral applications with disdain, disregarding any suggestion that these are elements worth being considered by enlightened twenty-first-century professionals. In fact, the very idea that we need to return to instilling historic Judeo-Christian values and standards to any area of public life is, to them, downright dangerous.

The descent of a God-fearing culture to one that is aggressively anti-Christian was not a phenomenon born overnight. There were, in fact, several degenerative stages that have brought us to where we are now. The culture has moved rapidly from that aforementioned blissful era of innocence to the entrenched menace of the aggressive godlessness, cynicism, and anti-God militancy strangling the nation in this new millennium. And, again, the core breakdown can be traced directly to our culture's making a deliberate choice to turn from God.

> Until the late 1980s, organized religion enjoyed the highest confidence of the American public, leading all other institutions in which they had a great deal of confidence. Two out of three Americans named the church as an institution in which they placed the utmost trust. Today, slightly more than half of all Americans say they place great trust in organized religion, which makes the military and police the institutions most trusted by Americans....[Furthermore], about half of Americans who say they are religious and consider spirituality important in their life attend religious services less than once a month or never.[7]

Echoes from the Sacred Book

This unfortunate scenario is not new to the realm of societies that formerly held fast to true religion. The truth is, the pattern is cyclical, and for those who care to pay attention, it is immensely instructive.

The Old Testament is replete with stories of ancient Israel's repeated bouts with straying from the dictates and worship of the one true God. In every case, their plunges into self-indulgence, love of lucre, idolatry, fornication, and alliances with pagan neighbors initiated catastrophic consequences. These excursions were remedied only by national repentance and turning back to Jehovah. New Testament history tells a similar story and pinpoints the problems in the opening chapter of the epistle to the Romans.

"When they knew God..." (Romans 1:21). This statement is a telling indictment against nations and cultures enlightened with the knowledge of the supreme Sovereign of the universe and their obligation to exercise allegiance and fidelity to Him alone.

"...they glorified him not as God..." (Romans 1:21). In other words, there came a time when these people who had known Him refused to give Him His place, and like their spiritual forbears at the ancient Tower of Babel, they decided to take matters into their own hands and chart a course clearly divergent from God's specific commands.

"...neither were thankful..." (Romans 1:21). Relishing their self-sufficiency, they developed a well-honed attitude of ingratitude and an arrogant disregard for any recognition of the need for dependence on their Creator.

"Professing themselves to be wise, they became fools..." Erudition in innumerable fields of economic, technical, and intellectual endeavor brought a total collapse of any fidelity to God and the inviolable truths of His Word. In short, these accomplished secularists made the final and decisive break with all of the values and moral commitments of their forefathers. In the end, they despised even retaining these hallowed memories in their minds.

"...*and changed the glory of the uncorruptible God...*" (Romans 1:23). The new order demanded change—change simply for the sake of change, not unlike the young arsonist at Columbia University who burned academic buildings only to see what would rise out of the ashes. One thought alone prevailed: anything is better than what was enshrined in the past and had shaped the nation. It was a philosophy born of radical rejectionist commitment. They had made the devastating descent to pure hedonistic paganism.

"...*who changed the truth of God into a lie, and worshiped and served the creature more than the Creator...*" (Romans 1:25). The inevitable consequence of this disastrous sequence is the embrace of creature worship, in which man becomes center and circumference of the universe. It is narcissism in its purist humanistic form, with zero tolerance for any who dare to challenge what's happening.

Sad to say, what we read in Romans 1 could well be used to describe the story of contemporary America.

Judge Robert H. Bork said it well:

> Some of the most acute observers have thought that religion is essential to the health of American culture and, perhaps, to the survival of our democratic institutions. Most of these commentators viewed religion as the basis of morality, which is fundamental to all else. It is significant, then, that religion was seen as secure and central to American life in the nineteenth century but has appeared increasingly problematic in the twentieth....While the law permits Americans to do as they please, religion prevents them from contemplating, and forbids them to commit, what is rash or unjust. Americans hold religion to be indispensable to the maintenance of republican institutions. Despotism may govern without faith, but liberty cannot.[8]

CHAPTER TWO

A Christian martyr is one who chooses. Chooses to suffer death rather than to deny Christ... sacrifices something very important to further the Kingdom of God...endures great suffering for Christian witness.

THE VOICE OF THE MARTYRS

Not Quite
Made in America

THE "UGLY AMERICAN" IS THE SCORNED CARICATURE often bantered about by some people in Europe. Throngs of such ugly Americans have long enjoyed invading the Continent flaunting too much money, too much loud and indelicate conversation, gaudy apparel, and far too many odious comments about the superiority of everything done or made in the U.S.A. To many on the other side of the Atlantic, the total effect of imports from the premier fractious breakaway colony has seemed unseemly in the extreme. Bawdy music, violent and uncouth entertainment, combined with financial affluence, military superiority, and a number-one ranking in the international arena cause more than a little grumbling from the street on up to the statehouses of European capitols.

We know, of course, that not all Americans are "ugly Americans." We are also aware that much of what is reflected in American culture has its roots in what Europe has sent to us. Thus, in many respects, we are the products of our inheritance—an inheritance that has contributed to the cultural revolution now so sorely afflicting this Republic.

For example, we have Austria to thank, or blame, for sending us the mental meanderings of Sigmund Freud (1856–1939), the man who is touted the founder of psycho-analysis. He taught the susceptible that religious teachings best be viewed as neurotic relics, and that, when all is said and done, God is nothing more than an exalted, human-type father. Many deemed "intellectuals" were enthralled with Freud's fixation with human processes and animosity toward historic biblical beliefs—so much so that the German author Thomas Mann wrote in the *New York Times* (June 21, 1939), "The Freudian theory is one of the most important foundation stones for the edifice to be built by future generations, the dwelling of a freer and wiser humanity."

A second significant import was the blasphemous all-out war on the integrity of the Scriptures by the ill-named "higher critics." Briefly stated, these pseudotheologians set to work to dismantle the Word of God and create a culture dominated by agnosticism, which, in actuality, devolved into functional atheism. The entire movement can probably be best summarized in the teachings of the German existentialist Rudolph Karl Bultmann (1884–1976). Bultmann's claim to fame is to have reduced the New Testament, with the exception of the Passion, to a total myth. He is, therefore, remembered as the champion of "demythologization." In other words, Bultmann and a cadre of fellow scoffers sent us the notion that the Bible is fabricated irrelevance, and that we'd best consign it to the trash heap and move on to more intellectually liberating pursuits.

England exported the revolutionary teachings of Charles Darwin (1809–1882). His book, *On the Origin of the Species by Means of Natural Selection*, gave secularists in the scientific community a bible on which to dignify the idea that man is no more than a higher form of animal life. Eventually this theory, based more on faith than fact, became accepted as the rational alternative to biblical beliefs and the existence of God, particularly in the realm of the creation. Tepid attempts to make Darwin more palatable came in forms akin to theistic evolution, which posited that a supreme being initially spun the wheel and then left the premises. This slightly watered down version of the original Darwinian theory, though eagerly embraced by some liberal theologians, was actually a slightly burnished brand of the deism held by Thomas Jefferson and other founding fathers.

While much more could, of course, be written on each of these foreign imports, it is enough to say that together they formed the siege engines assaulting historic biblical, theological, and social mores long held by the vast majority of Americans. In the end, these bastions of unbelief have had a withering impact on the whole of our society. And rather than, as adherents claim, reinforcing the premise that humanity is evolving upward, these abhorrent theories have combined to contribute to a grand demonstration of the essential fact of the depravity of the human species. Thus they have ushered into Western society a neopaganism that has fallen upon us with devastating results. The cultural revolution that devotees have gleefully fostered in this country has brought us to a time when we are beginning to reap the whirlwind. And Americans are not the only casualties.

The New Face of Britain

In his thought-provoking book *The Abolition of Britain from Winston Churchill to Princess Diana,* author Peter Hitchens articulates the deepening problems of the cultural revolution commonly shared by England and America. One reviewer commented, "Peter Hitchens has put his finger on a deep unease. Away from London, in the villages, among the old, the retired, country-dwellers, farmers and landowners, people are unhappy. They feel that the New Britain is out to get them."[9]

And, indeed, conservative American cousins on the other side of the Atlantic share this feeling. A summary passage speaks to the issue of intellectuals considering themselves progressive liberals in this generation.

> This is the joy of being a progressive. Whenever your views are rejected by experience, common sense and tradition, it is because you are ahead of the rest of the population, never because you are eccentric or wrong or just plain arrogant, or because they are not convinced by your arguments. They will catch up, and if not, so much the worse for them.[10]

Expanding on that all-too-familiar declaration is a statement drawn from the Reith lectures popular in British universities and with the British Broadcasting Company.

> Two sets of Reith lectures, chosen and promoted by the BBC, gave currency and respectability to new ideas about the family. Professor Edmund Leach, an anthropologist, shocked a still-conventional audience with several passages in his broadcasts, "A Runaway World?" in 1967. His opening was aggressively post-Christian: "Men have become like gods; isn't it about time that we understood our divinity?" It is also openly relativist. Leach simply did not accept that there were any absolute rules outside time and space. Everything was up for negotiation, like the salary or the price of a house: "Morality is specified by culture; what you ought to do depends on who you are and where you are."[11]

Hitchens brought his thesis down to street level in comparing the immense changes in England between the time of

Sir Winston Churchill and the canonized late Princess Diana. By contrasting events surrounding the funerals of the late prime minister and the pop culture idol of the masses, he deftly identifies the massive changes that have taken place in England between 1965 and 1997.

> On the morning of Churchill's funeral, the crowds, friendly and considerate, [were] united by a common loss....Churchill's death, at the age of ninety, was peaceful and came as no surprise. The grief, therefore, was the gentle sorrow of farewell, rather than the fierce and partisan mourning of sudden and seemingly unjust bereavement...Churchill was certainly not universally loved...yet they would have respected him, and acknowledged that national mourning was fitting and proper. But even these mild malcontents were a minority of a minority.
>
> In 1997 there were uncounted millions who felt that the mourning for Princess Diana was overblown and unjustified...they did not welcome the unending coverage on TV and radio, they did not rejoice in the Prime Minister's role in the obsequies, they did not want to sign any book of condolence or take flowers to Kensington...they had doubts about the taste of Elton John's performance in the Abbey, they dislike the applause and the flash of cameras, which marked the passing of the Princess's coffin. Great numbers of such people, for the most part those who could remember [Churchill] and 1965, were, however, silent.
>
> The society they now lived in, where the word of television was law, suddenly allowed only one point of view, and it was not theirs....More astute social conservatives realized that the lens of television was sending society a picture of itself that was simultaneously flattering, dishonest and designed to encourage

only one set of ideas about what is good—in politics, humour, architecture, foreign affairs, charity, fashion, education, and morals.[12]

A nation fed by TV, sound bites, and pop idol frenzy has taken the bait. This shallowing of England is a twin sister to the paper-thin perceptions of millions of Americans whose chief sources of information are rap lyrics and late-night TV.

The New National Reality

In many respects religion, though hardly regarded a major influence today, was the most significant battleground in the struggle to create a new national reality. Those self-proclaimed "progressives" who sought a seat on the bandwagon built by the higher critics, Darwin cultists, and Freudian cynics felt decidedly embarrassed by the dogmas and strictures of traditional religion and worship forms. Upscale clerics wanted "change." And it wasn't long in coming.

According to Peter Hitchens,

> Hell was abolished around the same time that abortion was legalized and the death penalty was done away with....After all, nobody went to Hell any more, did they? For by the 1960s, eternal damnation, like most of the more worrying aspects of the Christian religion, had apparently fallen into disuse. Bishops... had begun to admit, rather coyly to start with, that they were not sure about the existence of God or the truth of their religion's central beliefs.[13]

Consequently, religious leaders were faced with a question:

> How was it [religion] to become "relevant" to the new age without becoming completely irrelevant to its purpose of saving souls?[14]

> When there are no souls to be saved, only bodies—
> women and "kids"—there is only one object: to make
> living conditions better, even if they then grow up—as
> they often do—in grave moral poverty....If you do
> not believe in sin, then you can hardly be expected to
> use up much energy fighting against it. And if you do
> believe in sin, then you are "judgemental," and auto-
> matically excluded from the debate.[15]

What the dilemma confirms is the headlong plunge by the mainline denominations both in Britain and, correspondingly, the United States, into the realm of, in the words of the apostle Paul, "another gospel." In this case "the social gospel" which emphasizes working for human betterment minus the indispensable spiritual message of the new birth and transformation of life through becoming a "new creature" in Christ. The ironic result, now clearly in evidence, was that in their frantic rush toward relevancy, the mainliners actually made themselves irrelevant—something they neither understood, nor would they accept the admonition to "return to their first love." To add insult to injury, the phenomenal rise of evangelical churches, while the major denominations were experiencing rapidly diminishing memberships, helped fuel the animosity that would crescendo into the categorical denunciation of the much maligned "religious right"—a topic we will further explore in another chapter.

Liberal social engineering brought "progressive" education into the British system with the same unabashed fervor introduced in the United States. Corporal punishment, rote learning, religious training, traditional norms for classroom discipline and structure went by the boards. The socialism gripping the political system with its passion for leveling society was no less apparent in the halls of learning. Conservative ways of doing things was viewed as quite out of step with the march toward a secularly fashioned new world order.

Hitchens counters:

> Proper education is a fundamentally conservative activity, based on the assumption that a body of knowledge exists, is in the hands of the adult and educated, and can be passed on in measurable ways, by disciplined learning reinforced with authority.[16]

The refusal to adhere to these basic elements, wherever instigated, brings about predicable results.

> In the years since Bridget Plowden's report [Plowden Report of 1967] encouraged the spread of discovery learning and began the bonfire of old-fashioned desks and blackboards, children in this country have changed completely. Many cannot read, write, or count, many more can only do these things badly. Standards of behavior, of self-control, of ability to respond to authority or concentrate on any task have sunk. Other forces, such as television or the decline of the family, can also be blamed for this. However, the schools, which could have put the brake on the decline, have speeded it up.[17]

> A third major contributor to the cultural revolution in the United Kingdom is that much maligned—too often rightly so—box in the corner of dens and living rooms—the television. While it can be said that television brings many uplifting programs and documentaries into our homes, and is potentially a magnificent source of culture and learning, negative aspects go far to offset the benefits.

> Come to television as an adult, literate and independent, and it may make you lazy and passive, but it cannot leech away the thoughts, memories and imagination you already possess. But what if you come to it

as a tiny child, your memory undeveloped, and your imagination a blank space, your social and conversational abilities as yet non-existent? Is it possible that you will be a different *kind* of person from your parents?[18]

The answer to that rather obvious rhetorical question is, of course you will. And this is one of the major factors in how, in a generation, the whole of history can be altered, and the progressive cultures of once-great nations put in reverse and very literally turned upside down.

What Peter Hitchens's comments have documented in a striking way is the undeniable pervasiveness of a new reality that is not made in America or isolated to our culture. The danger is real and universal in the Western world. There is a devouring malignancy eating away at everything we have treasured, fought for, and died to preserve in our countries. And while the whole of our society can, in one respect, be viewed as a casualty, it is evangelical Christians who are bearing the brunt of the attack and being dealt out of the process.

Chapter Three

Thus was he three quarters of an hour or more in the fire. Even as a lamb, patiently he abode extremity thereof, neither moving forwards, backwards, nor to any side: but he died as quietly as a child in his bed. And now he reigneth, I doubt not, as a blessed martyr in the joys of heaven, prepared for the faithful in Christ before the foundations of the world; for whose constancy all Christians are bound to give praise.

Master John Hooper
England, 1555

Parallel Persuasions

THE NEW SECULAR HUMANIST THEOLOGY that has, in recent decades, become more firmly entrenched in the United Kingdom has also taken root here in the United States, attracting many adherents to heed its precepts. And many mainline Protestant churches eagerly joined the procession in the descent into the spiritual vacuum. While it would take years for many of their constituents to even get a whiff of what was happening, their well-heeled leaders were in the vanguard of the descent into theological irrelevance. And although their leadership did not yet grasp it, they were canceling themselves out as significant players in the arena of future events. And the effect on these mainline churches?

> The typical congregant at a liberal church...finds it increasingly hard to see why he should spend his Sunday morning...in a place where secular views are simply echoed.
> Weigh the benefits. Sunday with the family at the beach or in church listening to a sermon on AIDS; working for overtime wages or enduring pious generalities about "dialoguing," "inclusiveness," and "sharing

and caring"; studying for exams or hearing that the consolations and promises of the Bible are not "really" or "literally" true. Liberal Protestantism has succeeded in making itself dispensable.[19]

Thus the same debilitating forces ravishing Great Britain have created a parallel situation in the United States. This parallelism gives rise to the conclusion that the secular revolution is a plague throughout the Western world, and the struggle that has ensued is serious, deeply consequential, and dangerous. Judge Robert H. Bork, regarded by many as America's most distinguished conservative scholar, summarized well the effects of the teachings of Freud, Marx, and Darwin:

> It was tempting for men who wanted freedom from religious prohibitions to accept the idea that science was steadily disproving religious claims. The three most influential thinkers of the modern era, men who advanced their theories as science, either were bitterly hostile to religion or espoused theories that could be read to undercut faith. Sigmund Freud assailed religion "in all forms as an illusion and therefore recast it as a form of neurosis." Karl Marx viewed religion as superstition that opposed the progress of the working class. Charles Darwin offered the theory of evolution that was taken by many to disprove the theory of a Creator. Many people were particularly attracted to what they took to be the message of the new science of psychology: sex is the driving force of life and inhibitions are not only passé but dangerous.[20]

As we shall discover, the most acute danger experienced as the secular revolution evolved would be to evangelical Christians and others committed to traditional religious beliefs, values, and practices.

The Secularization of the Church

A popular perception is that America is a religious country, dedicated, at least in general respects, to Judeo-Christian concepts. In one respect, statistics would seem to bear this out. It is reported that 90 percent of Americans profess belief in God. Approximately one-half say they pray a least once a day, and some 40 percent claim to have attended church in a given week. This sounds well and good, but the facts of life in the country and more carefully mapped statistics tell quite another story.

> The truth is that, despite the statistics on churchgoing, etc., the United States is a very secular nation that, for the most part, does not take religion seriously. Not only may the statistics overstate the religious reality—people may be telling pollsters what they think makes a good impression—but statistics say nothing of the quality and depth of American religious belief. It is increasingly clear that very few people who claim a religion could truthfully say that it informs their attitudes and significantly affects their behavior.[21]

In *Factual Overview: Religion in America,* former Secretary of Education William Bennett reports that "about half of the Americans who say they are religious and consider spirituality important in their life attend religious services less than once a month or never."[22]

And when Americans *do* attend our churches, what do they hear?

The few times I attended church services during my youth in our small town, it happened to be at the dominant mainline denominational church in the community. The preacher, an affable "modernist" of the first order, prided himself in short homilies devoid of any references that might cause parishioners to squirm in their pews. Most were feel-good book reviews given to congregants who had no intention of reading them for themselves. The minister's main claim to fame was that he was a fine "sock hopper." This gift for the weekend dance among the young people in the Fellowship Hall made him an immensely popular figure among parishioners. What I, and most of the members of the congregation, didn't realize was exactly what was taking place. Although there were some older members who remembered the days when former pastors breathed the fire of the gospel during their sermons, challenged the lost to salvation and believers to a deeper walk with God, the younger churchgoers did not. What few realized was that this man was the first of the revolutionaries dedicated to changing the face of religion in our town. He was successful. Until this day that church has been in a process of spiritual digression. So much so that like the whole of the liberal religious establishment, it has faded into a state of superficial irrelevance.

Judge Bork makes this telling observation:

> The mainline Protestant churches have melded too much with the secular culture so that their members see less reason to attend. It would be more accurate to say that these churches have melded with the far left wing of the secular culture. The decline in membership would be even more dramatic if parishioners were aware of just how extreme many of the church bureaucracies have become.[23]

Unbeknown to the naïve and bureaucracy-trusting members of the aforementioned small-town mainline church, their smiling new-wave pastor was not just delivering them from the "ministerial stodginess" of the past, he was deliberately leading a rebellion against the sacred truths his denomination had been founded to propagate, and, in more ways than one, they were picking up the tab.

> The late Christopher Lasch, who was by no means a conservative, asked "what accounts for the [our society's] wholesale defection from the standards of personal conduct—civility, industry, self-restraint—that were once considered indispensable to democracy?" He answered that a major reason is "the gradual decay of religion." Our liberal elites, whose "attitude to religion," Lasch said, "ranges from indifference to active hostility," have succeeded in removing religion from public recognition and debate.[24]

What most of the people in the pew didn't have an inkling of was that the men to whom they had entrusted their spiritual welfare were courting catastrophe. And it wasn't a matter of their going in as innocents unaware. These people had an agenda. They had repudiated the faith of their fathers and mothers and were creating a religious environment totally foreign to former generations. At the expense of what had taken centuries to build, they went dutifully about the business of destroying it. And like the 1960s collegiate arsonist at Columbia, they too were waiting to see what would rise out of the ashes. That was the reality, but they thought about their demolition crusade in slightly different terms. These willfully deluded practitioners of change for the sake of change thought they had the tools to construct a new state of religion—one that was humanity based, tolerant, and marked by liberation from the old ways. One of the most obvious rubs was in the fact that this "toleration" reached out only to those whom these proponents found tolerable. And Bible believers were simply not in the "tolerable" class.

Judge Bork rather emphatically expressed the basic function of what is at stake.

> Only religion can accomplish for a modern society what tradition, reason, and empirical observation cannot. Christianity and Judaism provide the major premises of moral reasoning by revelation of the stories in the Bible. There is no need to attempt the impossible task of reasoning your way to first principles. Those principles are accepted as given by God.[25]

In other words, to forsake biblical revelation, absolutes, values, morals, and ethical norms leaves society in general and individuals in particular without a chart or compass by which to maintain direction and a grasp of what is waiting at the ultimate destination. And to be adrift in a world where marauding paganism, cruelty, and barbarism are becoming the stuff of life in the new world order is a frightening prospect.

Swimming Out of the Mainstream

The larger tragedy is that at a time when the clear teaching of the Bible is desperately needed, the message of mainline churches has not only been muted. Rather, it has become hostile to the Christianity it claims to represent. In the context of biblical Christianity, it is strange to hear "Christian" clergymen championing the most virulent radical causes. David Klinghoffer comments,

> That when denominations endorse homosexual ordination and gay marriage, laud Roe v. Wade, invoke the blessing of the Greek earth goddess Gaia on women's conferences, featuring the veneration of "Sophia, Creator God," or borrow rites from other

religions such as the American Indian tobacco ritual, they are swimming out of the mainstream.[26]

Not only are the mainliners "swimming out of the mainstream" when it comes to providing any moral compass for the nation, they have become bedfellows with the most notorious radical movements and regimes on the face of the earth—and consequently have made a major contribution to the spiritual and moral breakdown of the culture. The results have been devastating.

Where Is the Voice of the Prophet?

No longer is the voice of the prophet calling the nation to repentance heard in the land. The very idea of such an intolerable and bigoted presumption—that there is any need for or right to call for repentance—is scorned as a thoroughly Neanderthal and odious concept. The situation reminds one of the days of ancient Israel, when the same pendulum swings between faith and failure were transpiring.

When Jeremiah the prophet was bringing the word of the Lord to King Zedekiah, warning the king of the impending defeat of Israel at the hands of the Babylonians, the religious "mainliners" who advised the king were less than pleased with what God had to say. This cadre of advisers, who spent their lives telling the king and his subjects what they thought he and they wanted to hear, were so offended by the prophet's forthright message that they repudiated, slapped around, and tossed the hapless prophet into prison. His crime: telling the truth. The nation was in fact in great peril, but the religious "feel good" merchants in the court were inclined toward pitching fantasy rather than hard reality.

In the midst of the entire fiasco there is a word that spoke volumes about that situation and also what is occurring in our own time: "Then Zedekiah, the king, sent, and took him out; and the king asked him secretly in his house, and said, Is there any word from the Lord? And Jeremiah said, There is…" (Jeremiah 37:17). His message was not what the king or his failed counselors would like to have heard, but it was what needed to be said. Thus that king was prepared for the inevitable period of coming captivity.

The word for us is that the Lord does, in every age, and regardless of how dire the circumstances become, raise up those who will "stand in the gap" and tell the truth regardless of the personal cost.

As mainstream Protestant leaders turned their backs on the authority of Scripture and the proclamation of the gospel and espoused radical liberal agendas, evangelical Christian groups began to emerge. Strong non-affiliated churches started filling the spiritual void in the lives of people who were asking the question Zedekiah posed to the prophet: "Is there a word from the Lord?" Evangelical publishing houses and hundreds of Christian radio stations and television outlets began drawing massive numbers of adherents, all to the chagrin of the former pontiffs of religious life in the United States. Those leaders who for much of the history of the country had been sought out on virtually every issue in our national life slipped into the unenviable position of being little more than shrill voices coming from the sidelines. Or, as we noted earlier in David Klinghoffer's words, "Liberal Protestantism has succeeded in making itself dispensable." And, we might add, spiritually irrelevant.

This, of course, is not the end of the story. The very success of the evangelical movement fostered a vengeful reaction from the discredited liberal religious establishment that, for all practical purposes, was a declaration of war. In a sense, a comparison can be drawn from what has taken place in Russia with the collapse of Communism and the freedom for evangelical elements outside the Orthodox establishment to propagate the Christian faith. Rather than welcome the influx of mission agencies and Christian workers from abroad as well as the emergence of underground Russian congregations, the Orthodox hierarchy reacted with resentment and opposition. A common front against evangelicals was forged with some of the most radical elements in and out of the Russian government. The souls of a people tyrannized by seven decades of Communist ineptitude and brutality was not the issue. At stake was the power to control and monopolize religious mechanisms. It was more about religious politics than declaring the eternal truths of God's Word. With ever-diminishing numbers at their disposal, rather than join in the proclamation of a dynamic gospel, the Orthodox hierarchy retreated into forms of aggression designed to mute the voices of those who did.

In America, piqued liberals plunged headlong into the mainstream of the secular cultural revolution and joined forces with those most vociferously opposed to evangelicals, whose message was resonating at the grassroots and in the country's political establishment. Being on the sidelines during the Herculean spiritual struggles looming on the horizon was exchanged for being once again in a mainstream of sorts. It was, however, the wrong stream for designated keepers of the souls of men and women. What liberal religionists had accomplished was foretold in the writings of the apostle Paul: "Professing themselves to be wise, they became fools" (Romans 1:22).

The War Within

The ensuing conflict that endures with ever-increasing intensity to this day is an immeasurably costly affair. The woefully inadequate liberal/humanist delusion that man is basically good is exacting an unimaginable price in bloodshed and shattered lives. Freudian psychology, mantled in the guise of Christian theology, suffers the delusion that there is no longer good and evil. There are only the normal and the sick human beings. And "most destructive [is] the belief that people are basically good leads to the conclusion that people need to feel accountable for their behavior only to themselves, not to God or to a religious code higher than themselves.[27]

The most tragic element in this commitment is that redemption is no longer a viable option. In other words, men and women are no longer in need of a Savior; they are perfectly capable of going it alone and making life decisions wholly compatible to what they conceive to be good or bad, right or wrong.

This was brought home to me in an extremely vivid manner some years ago when I was auditing a class in pastoral psychology in a Baptist seminary. At the time, that institution was a theological mixed bag. Outstanding theological scholars were members of a faculty laced with new wave liberals.

On one occasion, a minister from the "old school" was brought in to share a message at the morning chapel session. The man commendably spoke of the blood and the efficacy of the suffering of Christ for us all. When those of us in the pastoral psychology class returned to our classroom, the professor made an extended display ridiculing the message of the morning and attempting to impress the students with just how ludicrous it was to speak of blood being shed for our redemption or, indeed, the necessity of being redeemed at all. To his way of thinking, blood sacrifice was a totally pagan and outmoded concept—one that he was deeply offended to hear about or even know had been presented before impressionable candidates for the ministry.

This "professor" was not, in any sense of the word, a biblical Christian. He was a thoroughgoing Freudian who was totally hostile to Orthodox Christian beliefs. The tragedy was that this man was greatly admired by the young men in that class who would one day stand in the pulpits of that denomination.

From this professor's perspective (and in the eyes of those who think like him), those who believe and dare to propagate the timeless message of that chapel speaker are viewed as entrenched enemies of "mainline" Christian thinking. Not only that, they are also seen as obstacles in the way of the march to the new Utopia, and, therefore, necessarily expendable. They just don't fit in the modern, liberal scheme of things.

CHAPTER FOUR

We rest on thee our Shield and our Defender,
Thine is the battle, Thine shall be the praise
When passing through the gates of pearly splendor
Victors, we rest with thee through endless days.

Sung by JIM ELLIOT, NATE SAINT, ROGER YOUDERIAN,
PETE FLEMING, AND ED McCULLY
days before being martyred by the Aucas in 1956

Zero Tolerance

WHEN EVANGELICAL CHRISTIANS ARE broad-brushed as people who are waging religious warfare against the American culture, conspiring to dictate every detail of personal lifestyles and oppressing those with alternate views, it can only mean one thing: There is serious trouble ahead.

If we are to understand properly the truly revolutionary aspects of the cultural revolution in America, we must begin by acknowledging that in the new arrangement, evangelical Christians are looked upon as the odd man out. In a society professing to be bowing at the shrine of unfettered tolerance, there is zero tolerance for evangelicals, their Bibles, God, Christ, moral values, or commitment to divine absolutes. This says at least two things:

1. Evangelical Christians are rapidly becoming an endangered and disenfranchised minority.

2. This post-Christian culture is descending into chaos that will ultimately endanger the survival of our democracy and our very way of life.

Although such statements may come as a shock to culturally assimilated professing Christians, the hard facts are too well documented to ignore.

Among the most outrageous but revealing manifestations of what has been stated is the political strategy allegedly planned in the Democratic campaign to unseat President George W. Bush. An article in *World* magazine explains:

> How will Democrats campaign against a president whose approval ratings are in the upper 80s? The answer: Steal the war issue from the Republicans by scapegoating the "religious right," presenting conservative Christians as the moral equivalent of the Taliban....
>
> The new hostility to orthodox Christianity goes beyond considerations out of public policy. It aims at the theological content of Christianity, the very substance of the faith: that salvation comes through Jesus Christ.
>
> What galls the new anti-Christian bigots is evangelism. Even the private conviction that one has been saved by Christ implies that there is something wrong with all of the other ways by which people try to save themselves. The first stage of overt persecution would be "Anti-proselytizing laws," which already exist in several countries (including, in particular, Islamic countries).[28]

That unscrupulous politicians target evangelicals as insufferable bigots is not new or earth shaking. The fact that they feel confident enough to even plan such a strategy, however, says much about how far we have come in this country. It is a manifestation that mirrors the pervasive indifference toward the hundreds of thousands of Christians being martyred in a number of places around the world today.

A Lack of Interest?

On May 27, 2001, Martin and Gracia Burnham, veteran missionaries under the New Tribes Mission agency, were kidnapped along with a Philippine nurse from the Dos Palmas Resort on the Philippine Island of Palawan. Their captors were a shadowy group of Islamic rebels with links to the infamous al Qaeda terrorist Osama bin Laden. For a year the Burnhams languished in the jungles under the most severe conditions. During their incarceration, Martin, 42, contracted malaria, and the terrorists who were demanding ransom beheaded another American tourist in the group of captives.

On June 7, 2002, after the Burnhams had been captives for a full year in the jungle, Philippine troops located and stormed the terrorists' camp. In the ensuing shootout, Martin Burnham was killed and his wife, Gracia, wounded in the leg. Following her evacuation, Mrs. Burnham was flown to Kansas City to be reunited with her three children.

Tragically, only brief notice was taken by the secular media, and very little reported in Christian publications or electronic media. The plight of Christians such as Martin and Gracia Burnham—suffering privation and martyrdom by the thousands—receives scant publicity in today's media. Judge Bork puts his finger on one of the problems:

> The other marginalizing factor to be mentioned is the hostility or indifference of the national media to religion. Despite the fact that religion is a major feature of American life, it is the subject of only 1 percent of the news stories on the four major networks and the national print press, and those are typically hostile.... Whenever religion comes in contact with politics or

public policy, as it frequently does, the news media reacts in three distinct ways, all negative. Reporters treat religion as beneath mention, as personally distasteful, or as a clear and present danger to the American way of life.[29]

If it is true that in the eyes of members of the Fourth Estate religion is not worth mentioning, personally distasteful, and a danger to the American way of life, we can understand why a hostile environment, particularly toward evangelicals, is being fostered among people who confine their information sources to the evening news and the morning paper. This attitude even carries over to some members of the judiciary who have fought to expunge anything Christian from the public landscape of the United States. Without a doubt, God—that is, the Judeo-Christian deity—is out of favor in many of the federal courtrooms of America.

There can be no doubt, says Judge Bork, that the systematic hostility of the courts to religion has lowered the prestige of religion in the public mind. Indeed, the message that any contact between religion and government—even a nonsectarian prayer at a school commencement—violates the document upon which our nation is formed can only send a message that religion is dangerous, perhaps sinister.[30]

A Growing Hostility

We are all familiar with the ludicrous lengths to which some members of the Supreme Court and judiciary will go to strain at the proverbial gnat while swallowing atheist camels. The Ten Commandments, mentioning Jesus in valedictory addresses, Christmas crèches in public squares, Christian or Jewish symbols in hallowed public buildings, thanking God for food in elementary lunchrooms, and other perceived absurdities, are what we have come to expect. But every once in a while the sleeping giant is ruffled enough to emit a roar, roll over, and then go back to sleep.

The giant was indeed ruffled when in June of 2002 a brash 49-year-old atheist lawyer named Michael Newdow took to the courtroom with a complaint about his eight-year-old daughter reciting the Pledge of Allegiance in her classroom. Newdow argued before a panel of the U.S. Court of Appeals in San Francisco that to keep his daughter unsullied by religious indoctrination, the words "under God" should be struck from the pledge. The panel agreed and ruled that the words "under God" were a violation of the Constitution, and should, therefore, be stricken from the document.

The mind-boggling decision caused a firestorm of reaction that reached all the way to the halls of Congress. Veteran Democrat Senator Byrd gave an impassioned speech in which he pointed out the lunacy of the judges' decision, going so far as to invite them to have him arrested and incarcerated for having himself recited the pledge in public. What was arresting about the senator's speech was the questions he posed. He first asked, "What has happened to this country?" He then followed that by querying, "Are we going to let a crowd of atheists take over America?"

The answers? First, a lot has gone wrong in the land of the free. And the court's ill-advised decision is symptomatic of the problem that is strangling freedom in America. And second, that is indeed what's happening. The radical vocal minority, including atheists and people at odds with virtually everything this nation has been built upon, are consistently winning the day. Unfortunately, in addition to the courts, they have plenty of help from major and influential segments of society.

Consider, for example, the entertainment industry and the treatment God-fearing people receive in their productions: "Christians are the only group Hollywood can offend with impunity, the only creed it actually goes out of its way to insult. Clerics, from fundamentalist preachers to Catholic monks, are routinely represented as hypocrites, hucksters, sadists, and lechers. The tenets of Christianity are regularly held up to ridicule."[31]

Walking in lockstep with the courts and entertainment industry are liberal Protestant church figures—in particular, the leaders of the National Council of Churches of Christ in America (NCC), the umbrella organization for U.S. mainline denominations.

The NCC has a history of romanticizing left-wing movements in the Third World. Thus any mention of the persecution of Christians in these countries must be balanced with an equal or excessive critique of some inequity toward minorities in the United States.

Referring to the NCC, Paul Marshall makes this observation:

> There is one other relevant trend, this one more specifically theological in nature. Many mainline church seminaries now tend to downplay any stress on the specific truths of Christianity. One of the major emphases has become openness to and dialogue with other religions and ideological movements. While dialogue and a critical openness is certainly to be welcomed, one of the results has been reluctance to raise anything which might damage peaceful relations with conversation partners. This also leads to an animus against people engaged in seeking to propagate their faith, with an implication that such troublemakers might deserve what they get. This means that the NCC doesn't seem to like evangelism (or "prosely-

tizing"), and is not very sympathetic to those who suffer it.[32]

Two other fellow travelers of these debunkers of things Christian are worthy of mention:

> Intellectuals, often self-appointed, have fallen in love with the pagan secular/humanist/scientific deity. They reflect the thought prevalent throughout the history of man that there is ample justification to go it alone. They see self as center and circumference of the universe and the mind as a major object of veneration. These people fancy that they need no god-crutch to make it through life. They can fend quite well for themselves, thank you: "The major obstacle to a religious renewal is the intellectual classes, who are highly influential and tend to view religion as primitive superstition. They believe that science has left atheism as the only respectable intellectual stance, routed the believers."[33]

And then there are the radical environmentalists, who, in their own way, seem to bring the convictions of the proponents of atheism to an inevitable and, yes, embraced conclusion. Jewish radio personality Dennis Prager expresses it well:

> As a result of this encounter, I have come to understand that part of the environmentalist movement is a protest against the Judeo-Christian elevation of the human species above other species. That explains the head of Earth First! declaring that human beings are a "cancer on the earth," and the head of People for the Ethical Treatment of Animals (PETA) comparing the barbecuing of six billion chickens with the killing of six million Jews. And it explains the movement against any use of animals for medical research.[34]

In a speech made at an animal rights conference in McLean, Virginia, a Princeton bioethicist argued that Christianity hurts animals. One of the things that causes a problem for the animal movement, said atheist professor Peter Singer, is the strong strain of

> fundamentalist Christianity that makes a huge gulf between humans and animals, saying humans have souls and animals do not....The Judeo-Christian ethic also teaches that humans are made in the image of God and that God has given mankind "dominion" over animals....This belief has a very negative influence on the way in which we think about animals.[35]

How Society Views Christians

You will have no doubt noticed that in major areas of the American culture orthodox religion and evangelical Christians are identified as a pox on the life of the people of the United States. There are those who proclaim that committed Christian believers are a clear and present danger to the country, a drag on human progress, a divisive millstone around the neck of a liberated society, and generally a crowd of undesirables fit only to be roundly repudiated.

A particularly concerning keynote struck by anti-Christian lobbyists is that which is directed against evangelism. Those missionaries, such as the Burhams, who have given their lives to the ministry of propagating the love and life of Christ to spiritually benighted people, when martyred, are written off as probably having received what they asked for. This makes for an extremely dangerous environment for evangelicals who are serious about the biblical commission to make Christ known.

These people, who veneer themselves with rhetorical tolerance for every kind and creed, are actually the most intolerant species on the face of the American landscape. They militantly promote the idea that every religion, cult, jungle paganist, and God-denying element is equally credible and acceptable in their own right. Those afflicted by the you're OK; I'm OK syndrome have declared the Christian message intolerable and at cross purposes with progress toward a religious global unity heralding a new world church—a less monolithic entity minus the debilitating strictures of the Bible, its God, or adherents to His mandates.

Thus when it is proposed by thinking people that we can expect movements in the future that will demand national laws against evangelizing, we can take their contention with more than a grain of salt. And if this becomes a fact of life in America, overt persecution will not be far behind.

Interestingly, Jewish journalists and commentators have been among the first to begin to sound the alarm. While this may seem strange to many Christians, given the history of the Jewish people, it is easy to understand. What they have been saying, in essence, is this: "You evangelicals had better wake up. We've seen all this before. When a segment of society is designated as an undesirable minority, sooner or later that society has to figure out what to do with these people. It is then that the trouble comes."

If this appears to be an overly pessimistic view, consider this. American Christians have been insulated for centuries against the types of persecution that have been true of believers in other eras and places. It is also true that we have been insulated from the bloody persecution currently affecting hundreds of thousands of our brethren in other countries. But when zero tolerance for the Christian message becomes more and more a part of our nation's system, true evangelicals will have no choice but to keep preaching, teaching, and living the message of the gospel. This will put the system and believers on an irreversible collision course.

One problem we American evangelicals have is that we have come to believe that the freedom, peace, and security we have enjoyed is a permanent and normal state with a lifetime guarantee. But take a good look around. It is a blessing virtually unparalleled in history, but it can be taken away.

> Certainly, mankind without Christianity conjures up a dismal prospect. The record of mankind *with* Christianity is daunting enough....The dynamism it has unleashed has brought massacre and torture, intolerance and destructive pride on a huge scale, for there is a cruel and pitiless nature in man which is sometimes impervious to Christian restraints and encouragements. But without these restraints, bereft of these encouragements, how much more horrific the history of these last 2,000 years must have been!...In the last generation, with public Christianity in headlong retreat, we have caught our first, distant view of a de-Christianized world, and it is not encouraging.[36]

Then why are the vast majority of evangelicals fast asleep?

CHAPTER FIVE

*They were stoned, they were sawn
asunder, were tested, were slain with the
sword; they wandered about in sheepskins
and goatskins; being destitute, afflicted,
tormented (Of whom the world was
not worthy)....*

HEBREWS 11:37-38

Insulation by Affluence

IN 1983, THE MUSLIM-DOMINATED GOVERNMENT in Khartoum declared Sudan, the largest country in Africa, an Islamic Republic. In 1991 Islamic law (*Shari'a*) was adopted and became the rule for all segments of the country's population. Commensurately, systematic suppression and genocide of non-Muslim religions accelerated to a degree not witnessed since the Nazi era. The primary targets were Nuba Christians living in the southern portion of the country.

Nina Shea reports:

> The militant Islamic government's scorched earth policy and forced starvation tactics as it prosecutes its religious war in the southern, Christian part of the country have resulted in the deaths of more than 1.3 million people and displacement of more than 34 million. [Estimates of deaths from some sources run as high as two to three million.] To eradicate the Christian and non-Muslim population, the Sudanese government and its agents have bombed, burned and looted southern villages; enslaved women and children; kidnapped and forcibly converted Christians and other

boys and sent them into battle; relocated entire villages into concentration camps called "peace villages"; and withheld food aid to starving Christians and animist communities until they converted to Islam.

Individual Christians, including clergy, have been assassinated, imprisoned, tortured, and flogged for their faith. There have been numerous reports of Christians being crucified in remote areas.[37]

Although the Sudan stands as a primary horror story of the persecution of Christians, relatively little has been said about it in the media or political circles. And most regrettably, nothing of any concrete or decisive nature has been done about it. What is most disconcerting is why Christians in the Western democracies have been silent. This question is raised in almost every significant report being produced on the issue of Christian persecution. Why are Christians, and in particular American evangelicals, silent, indifferent, or uninformed regarding this devastating scourge on fellow believers?

There can be no question that this generation of Christians is the best informed of any in the history of the world. Hundreds of television programs are beamed into homes with every passing week. Christian radio stations dot the landscape; innumerable publications come into the hands and homes of Christian families by the millions. Still, when it comes to serious programs or presentations of martyrs, murders, and mayhem, there is precious little being said or seen. Writing in the *Wall Street Journal*, Michael Horowitz wondered why, in the face of the immensity of the problem, it was for all practical purposes being ignored:

> America's Christian community is most directly challenged; its moral authority will be gravely tarnished if it fails to exercise its growing political influence on

behalf of people now risking everything to engage in the "simple" act of Christian worship and witness....[As a Jew] I am writing because I am pained and puzzled at the relative lack of interest shown by many within the Christian community of fellow Christians who are now increasingly persecuted—as Christians for their beliefs alone.[38]

Insulation by Affluence

Addressing reasons for this disconcerting state of malaise is a complex undertaking. But perhaps the fountainhead for what is taking place around us can be found in the unprecedented level of prosperity we have attained in America and the free world. In defense of American Christians, it can be said that the current state of affluence has been the source of huge benefits to efforts in world relief, missionary endeavor, propagation of the faith through multiple sources, academic institutions, and a plethora of other causes. At the same time, there has been a creeping state of assimilation into the culture that tends to desensitize many believers to the more unpleasant aspects of living the Christ life in a very bad world. For many decades Americans have been living on an island of peace and prosperity, but it is a haven that is rapidly shrinking.

This is, most certainly, nothing new. Others before us, most notably ancient Israel, have trodden the same path. After 70 years of captivity in Babylon, the ruling monarchs granted permission for the Jewish people to return to their homeland. The first wave followed Ezra the scribe, and their mission was to rebuild the Temple in Jerusalem. Approximately 100 years later, Nehemiah led a host of returnees to repair the walls around the city. Of the masses of Jewish people dwelling in Babylon at the time, only some 50,000 opted to go home. The rest chose to stay where they were. The reason was simple: Life was good in Babylon. It was too good to justify returning to a land that had been ravished and laid barren by invading armies and neglect. Facing hardship and uncertainty didn't seem to rank high on the Israelites' list of priorities. The clean streets of Babylon would do just fine, thank you.

In some respects, they were like Jewish people in the Northern Kingdom of Israel, who were known for their affluence and indifference:

> Woe to them who are at ease in Zion…that lie on beds of ivory, and stretch themselves upon their couches, and eat the lambs out of the flock, and the calves out of the midst of the stall; that chant to the sound of the harp, and invent to themselves instruments of music, like David; That drink wine in bowls, and anoint themselves with the chief ointments; but they are not grieved for the affliction of Joseph (Amos 6:1,4-6).

What the experience of ancient Israel—and the whole of humanity, for that matter—demonstrates is that it is extremely difficult to stay focused while swimming in a sea of affluence. The experiences of every great empire are a proof text. All seem to have moved along a curve: clawing the way up from poverty to prominence, gaining territory, wealth, plenty, and prestige, then slowly slipping into the morass of self-gratification and over-indulgence, finally experiencing decadence, decline, then often back to poverty.

The gist of the matter is that on the way up societies on the rise seem to have an outward look, a vision for something bigger, better, more prosperous. Once such societies have attained their goals, however, the look more often turns inward and tends to become self-oriented and preoccupied with possessions and maintaining the status quo.

Apply the pattern to Western Christianity in the twenty-first century. We are benificiaries of an industrial revolution that has carried us into a state of life our forebears could only dream of. Much of the rest of the world looks in wonderment, admiration, envy, or aspires to bring us down and take it all from us. Viewing things as they are, one must conclude that we Americans have been insulated by our affluence to the point that we must ask ourselves this question: Are we in a situation that will take us to a state like the church at Laodicia, saying, "I am rich, increased with goods, and have need of nothing," and never realize that spiritually we are, in the eyes of God, "wretched, and miserable, and poor, and blind, and naked?"[39]

Addressing the question of why there is a relative lack of interest in the plight of suffering brothers and sisters world-wide, the Reverend David Stavers, vice president of the Bible League, offered two reasons:

1. American Christians for the most part are not interested in anything that happens outside the boundaries of the United States, and in many cases outside the boundaries of their own little community.

2. American Christians have no experience of persecution or suffering for their faith which remotely resembles the experiences of many of our overseas brothers and sisters. It is difficult to empathize... many, many, many American Christians refuse to believe what is reported because it is so far outside their experience.[40]

Reverend Stavers is quite correct. Consider this happening to you, a family member, or a neighbor.

In December of 1994, a Nigerian Christian was accused of desecrating the *Qur'an* by using its pages for toilet paper. Even though a local court exonerated him, he was detained ostensibly for "security purposes." The day after Christmas an enraged mob of Muslim fanatics stormed the jail, overcame the guards, and dragged the man out of his cell. Once outside, he was beheaded, and his severed head carried triumphantly through the streets on a spike.[41]

Sadly, atrocities of this kind are all too common in countries where Christians are marked for extinction. But, of course, it is not true here. But that being the case, why is it that one would be hard pressed to find an evangelical church bulletin board anywhere in the United States depicting the need for action or even prayer on behalf of those who are suffering such harrowing experiences? And to our shame, how long has it been since Christians in solid, Bible-preaching churches have heard significant passages or statements from our pulpits that made any reference to these tragedies? Thankfully, there are notable exceptions. But the general climate running the length and breadth of the evangelical community is more silent than vocal. We must conclude that there are reasons for the deafening silence immersing so much of the church body.

Living the Good Life

While researching the self-esteem movement in order to write an article I decided to visit Christian bookstores and see what they were offering on the subject. Because I was traveling the country as a conference speaker at the time, I had the opportunity to evaluate bookstore stock in quite a broad cross section of America. My first impression, which is even more pronounced now, was that the sections offering Bible exposition, theology, and reference works were shrinking. I discovered that, at the time, four categories dominated the shelves of these shops.

The Inner Self

"How can I love anyone else until I have learned to love myself?" That phrase has long been a recurring refrain in many Christian publications and public testimonies in scores of meetings and seminars. Now there's nothing wrong with self-respect as a believer and Christ-esteem. But to promote the idea of self-obsession and self-adulation seemed totally out of step with biblical reality. And as I perused the contents of some of these books, a verse kept running through my mind: "Let nothing be done through strife or vain glory, but in lowliness of mind let each esteem others better than themselves" (Philippians 2:3).

In the arena of the self-esteemists, the diminishing of self for the welfare of others—putting them first—was a cardinal act of denial of first principles. Self was the center and circumference of life. Among the most heinous sins in the catalog was fracturing your self-esteem or that of anyone else. Such transgressors demeaned the jocular "everything, starting with you, is beautiful" credo. The problem is that those who are honest with themselves understand that, given the nature of humanity, they are not self-generating fountains of perpetual self-loving effervescence. But rather, they are sinners saved by God's condescending grace and who are in need of the daily nurture, assurance, forgiveness, and strength that is truly functional only when Christ alone is the object of our esteem. In other words, "How can I love anyone else until I learn to love Him?"

The Body Self

Next on the list of preferred reading material was a host of books and manuals related to shaping, toning, and tanning the physical body. These, with some rather bizarre renditions, had devotees eating and drinking some strange concoctions, believing it was the will of God for every believer to be healthy and ever free of debilitating illness. One book offered the key to success for living the biblically mandated 120 years by eating an assortment of nuts, berries, and array of nutritional herbal goods. Unfortunately, the author succumbed, as I recall, in his forties.

Exercise booklets, running manuals, and training regimes heralded themselves as the tools toward a healthy, exuberant life on this planet. Many church fellowship halls were occupied during the week by enthusiasts leaping about in leotards doing aerobics, Jesuscizing, and performing various other muscle-challenging endeavors. Eaters anonymous groups gathered in small circles to share the burden of overeager appetites and learn push-away procedures. Then there were the sales staffs formed among church members to sell vitamins, food supplements, and enriching and youth-inducing skin products. For many, servicing the body began to approach near fetish proportions.

This is not to imply that there is anything wrong with reasonable care in maintaining the body, proper eating habits, and physical fitness. However, equal care must be taken to see to it that the body does not become the first priority of a Christian's life. The apostle Paul had something to say about this: "For physical training is of some value, but godliness has value for all things holding promise for both the present life and the life to come" (1 Timothy 4:8 NIV).

The Prospering Self

Prominent among the new wave of literature being embraced by success-oriented evangelicals were works on how to score big in the here and now: "Every day, in every way, I'm getting better and better." These words articulated the life philosophy of Napoleon Hill, a man who started out selling little return attachments for car keys that would guarantee postage paid for any key rings lost by their owners. From that inauspicious beginning Mr. Hill rose to amass a multimillion dollar fortune and make a significant mark in the business world.

In my younger days I did a brief stint in the employ of one of the Hill insurance companies. Every meeting of the company began with the phrase, "Every day, in every way, I am getting better and better." In the context of the business we were serving, that power-of-positive-thinking mantra was translated into financial success. It was never, in our minds, associated with anything spiritual. It was simply a success formula that, if employed properly, would help you make a lot of money.

I was, therefore, rather taken aback to find Napoleon Hill's books—among many other similar works—on the shelves of Christian bookstores. I shouldn't have been. Financial success was clearly in the mainstream of the evangelical market. The primary idea transmitted seemed to be that God wants you rich, and that financial success is the direct result of the favor of God on your life. Many of the books were of the "name it and claim it" variety. The "grab the brass ring, you deserve it" motif was very much in vogue, and it still is. Big cars, big homes, opulent surroundings, large holdings, and bulging financial portfolios were the promised result of following the "seven steps to success" approach to affluence. As one would expect when it comes to matters of purse or pocket, some of the propositions presented were bizarre in the extreme. One prosperity gospel proponent made the claim that every believer had angels available to act as procurers of goods and services for them. The proof was claimed from the Psalms: "Bless the Lord, ye his angels, that excel in strength, that do his commandments, hearkening unto the voice of his word. Bless ye the Lord, all ye his hosts, ye ministers of his, that do his pleasure" (Psalm 103:20-21).

The assumption was that if the angels are obligated to do the bidding of God's word, and Christians use the word, then the angels are obligated to fill the requests of Christians.

Financial planning and success seminars were blossoming at an equal pace with the growth of financial possibilities available in a vibrant economy. One friend, speaking of a prominent financial planner, said, "You know, that fellow puts a dollar sign on every verse in the Bible."

The persistent difficulty with an excessive emphasis on financial prosperity is that it is virtually a made-in-America phenomenon. If one attempts to take the "name it and claim it" prosperity gospel message or philosophy to any Third World country and impose its principles, it simply won't work. In reality, such success-is-everything teaching demeans our credibility in a world that has none of these advantages. Try preaching it to the family of the Nigerian Christian whose head was being carried past their home at the end of a spike. It won't fly there.

The Sexual Self

The fourth category was devoted to sexuality and promised much more than you probably wanted to know. In an increasingly paganized culture that has become perpetually frenzied over sex and sexual excesses, it seems that many Christians are becoming desensitized to the standards of purity as presented in the Bible. Some of the book titles on the store shelf reflected a measure of the titillation that seems to be little more than a spillover from secular publications. On the second shelf of a Christian bookstore in Florida, within easy reach of children, was a large sex manual formatted to look like the secular *The Joy of Sex* publication. The Christian version was graphically illustrated and, frankly, could be categorized as salacious. It certainly was not what children should have access to in a "Christian" bookstore.

Is sexuality a part of life for Christians? Certainly. But exploiting sex for profit is another matter.

Keeping a Right Perspective

In summary we can ask ourselves: Is a healthy attitude toward one's self a good thing? Yes. Is maintaining good physical health and nutritional habits a good thing? Yes. Is a responsible handling of finances and the careful management of physical resources a good thing? Yes. Is developing a proper sexual equilibrium a good thing? Yes. Is having resources available a good thing? Yes.

However, when these subjects—or any others—cause us to lose our perspective of the larger issues facing the body of Christ worldwide, they are both wrong and dangerous. And, in the end, they contribute to our insulation by affluence. Or, we could say we end up becoming victimized by our own success. And, sadly, the greatest number of casualties impacted by this wave of secularized affluence are among those suffering and dying for their faith.

CHAPTER SIX

It was the Christian faith in the heart of the widow that brought forth kind and forgiving words for the murderers of her husband and two children. And it was also this faith that confronted the fatherless daughter to speak of a belief that brings solace in times of personal sorrow and tragedy.... [42]

SPOKEN OF GLADYS STAINES
after the martyrdom of her husband and two sons

Orphans in the Global Village

THE LATE FRANCIS A. SCHAEFFER MADE THIS observation about today's church:

> Does the church have a future in our generation?...I believe the church is in real danger. It is in for a rough day. We are facing present pressures and a present and future manipulation which will be so overwhelming in the days to come that they will make the battles of the last forty years look like child's play.[43]

In the heyday of the fundamentalist/modernist controversies of the first half of the last century, the great battles were in the fields of theology and dealt with the inerrancy of Scripture, evolution, the social gospel, and matters related more or less to the radical liberal departure from traditional orthodoxy. While we still confront residual issues in these areas, the lines have pretty well been drawn. The conflict today, one might say, has moved to the street. And we are grappling with what these conclusions have produced. Dr. Schaeffer wisely foresaw the "rough day" that was inevitable in a cultural setting severed from the moorings of biblical absolutes, stabilizing moral and ethical values, and the general restraints of Judeo-Christian order.

In an interesting way, the catalyst for exposing the fundamental issues marking the impassable gulf between serious evangelicals and liberal neopaganism is evangelism. The freedom to propagate one's faith openly among people with contrary beliefs and convictions was, in the past, a cherished principle in democratic systems—a given. This was certainly a basic fact of life for some 200 years of the American experience. Evangelicals, however, cannot take this for granted any longer. It is becoming increasingly and painfully clear that Christian evangelism has been given an eviction notice.

One of the more blatant illustrations of this came from the highest office in the land during the Clinton tenure in the White House. When the Southern Baptists announced plans to launch a campaign to share the gospel with Hindus and Muslims, they were condemned by the president. Speaking for Mr. Clinton, White House Press Secretary Joe Lockhart placed Baptists in the category of groups that "perpetuate ancient religious hatred."[44] The press secretary also leveled the charge that the great challenge of the twenty-first century would be to eliminate "intolerance...and religious hatred." Conservative evangelicals Craig and Janet Parshall rightly observed, "It is no overstatement to say that the Clinton administration's statements against the Southern Baptist view of the Great Commission represents one of the most outrageous White House attacks against evangelicals in our time."[45]

Camping with the Athenians

For reasons we shall explore, the prevailing mood is that every religion, cult, sect, or form of tribal ritualism is of equal value and should be accepted on its own terms. To presume, therefore, that Christianity is not simply another way but the only way to obtain eternal life and a right relationship with God is totally out of sync with contemporary humanistic enlightenment. Consequently, to propagate the gospel of the New Testament and make Christ known is regarded as an unspeakable affront totally unacceptable in this new land of many gods.

In many respects, we are revisiting the spiritual conditions experienced in the first century by the early emissaries of the Christian faith. In Athens the apostle Paul and his companions found themselves in an environment in which the philosophical heavy hitters "spent their time in nothing else, but either to tell, or to hear some new thing" (Acts 17:21). Those pagan denizens of Mars Hill in ancient Athens were engaged in the same quest as modern philosophers. Theirs was a search for truth that they never managed to find. To hear some new point that would titillate their intellect, some strange and novel concept, or a dark new mystery religion was the be-all and end-all of their daily lives.

It was a place of altars erected for the veneration of many gods, and these polished pagans deemed themselves to be religious in the extreme. In order to cover every base, they even erected an altar of particular interest to the apostle of Christ: "For as I passed by, and beheld your devotions, I found an altar with this inscription, TO THE UNKNOWN GOD. Whom, therefore, ye ignorantly worship, him declare I unto you" (Acts 17:23).

That message revolutionized the Western world and became the basis of the democracy that liberated whole nations from the strangulation, deprivation, and the barbarism centuries of jaded paganism had imposed. Now, it seems, we are experiencing a return to Mars Hill. Unfortunately, the journey is not an ascent to better things, but a digression into a neopagan culture eager to stifle the very message that set us free.

Orphans in the Global Village

When the term "the New World Order" came into the mainstream of the American vocabulary in the last decade of the twentieth century to describe the new direction our world was headed, few people actually understood the ramifications of the era we were entering. In short order, the "global village" was under construction and we were being reminded constantly for the need to retool our thinking to adjust to a radical new reality. The nation was, indeed, on the cusp of a "new reality," one that would require a radical change in thinking and lifestyles. The old nationalist mindset was being swept under the rug—a mindset that liberals perceived as one more piece of debris that was an obstacle to progress.

The light began to dawn when entire major industries began flying out of country and relocating on other shorelines along the Pacific Rim. Warnings from political figures such as presidential candidate Ross Perot about the "great sucking sounds" from abroad taking American jobs were brushed aside as old nonsense. America is now expected to merely be one cog in the international wheel and we're condemned when we attempt to protect our national interests. The New World Order was, in fact, more than liberal sloganeering; it was *the* force to be reckoned with. And in order for the cog to fit, we are expected to cater to a new set of priorities.

The Global Economy

The "money means everything" philosophy has not been difficult for pampered, secularized Western neopagans to accept. After all, following the cultural revolution, personal wealth and security were what life was *all* about. And the new prosperity fit the pattern perfectly. But there would be casualties, a fact that was dramatically illustrated when the American stock market took a major plunge in July of 2002.

Newscasts, print media, and economic analysts were panic stricken. Some commentators went so far as to compare the plunge to the crash of 1929. Others referred repeatedly to the anger in the streets of America over the corporate malfeasance of the Enrons, WorldCom, and their book-cooking accounting cohorts. A traumatizing concern was how all this would affect the United States's role as leader of the free world. How much was real and how much was partisan political rhetoric is debatable, but one thing was painfully evident: The situation ethics of no absolutes and every person operating along a "what's good for me track" and the greed sanctioned by a culture without moral and spiritual moorings was coming home to roost.

Do Americans still possess the capacity for outrage? Yes—at least, apparently, when it is a matter of money. But all through this financial markets debacle, I kept thinking of the hundreds of thousands of Christians, some of them Americans, who were bleeding and dying at the hands of bloodthirsty tyrants and fanatics in dozens of countries. I saw no appreciable show of outrage here. Most likely, part of the reason is that their plight has no impact on the country's wallet. In addition, moving against governments that tolerate and even encourage and participate in persecuting and killing innocent Christians might indeed have an adverse economic impact. The choice is obvious: Money wins the day. These Christians don't live on Main Street in the global village. But then didn't we hear something about this a couple of thousand years ago? "For the love of money is the root of all (kinds) of evil, which, while some coveted after, they have pierced themselves through with many sorrows" (1 Timothy 6:10).

In the book of Revelation, the imagery of the final destruction of ecclesiastical and commercial "Babylon" is dramatically portrayed. While there is some difference of opinion among trustworthy scholars about the precise interpretation of the text, at least two facts are very clear in this scene:

1. God is reaping divine judgment on a global system that has become totally degenerate and corrupt.
2. A great hew and cry is raised over the gigantic commercial calamity experienced in this judgment.

The "kings of the earth" are described as horrified witnesses of the event (verse 9). "Standing afar off for fear of her torment, saying, Alas, that great city, Babylon, that mighty city! For in one hour is thy judgment come. And the merchants of the earth shall weep and mourn over her; for no man buyeth their merchandise any more....The merchants of these things, who were made rich by her, shall stand afar off for the fear of her torment, weeping and wailing" (Revelation 18:10-11,15).

These kings and their merchant collaborators are not weeping about lost lives, collapsing social structures, or the broken lives and dreams of real people. Rather, they are lamenting the loss of wealth, delicacies, power, and the personal aggrandizement these things provide.

A secular television commentator said recently that a day was coming when wars would not be waged based exclusively on military considerations; he said wars of the future would be economic conflicts. We may not agree completely with this analysis, but we can venture the conclusion that future military confrontations will more likely be driven by economic expediency than humanitarian sensibilities. Bottom line: The name of the game in the global village is money.

The New Ecumenicity

The new scheme of things in the international community mandates a leveling process. The "have nations" must become "have less" entities, while "have not" nations move up to a "have more" status. In other words, inclusivism is the standard, with diverse components operating in harmony. It is actually a kind of global neosocialism. As we have observed, the unifying factor in the global structure is economic. When we move into the arena of religion, however, the centralizing consideration is unity.

The kind of unity set in this environment is not built on the old ecumenical model of the last century. In those days, upscale Protestant religionists came together with the idea of inter-denominational cooperation based on liberal interpretations of theology. Everything deemed divisive and offensive would be set aside in favor of a social action offensive. It goes without saying that the offensive elements tagged for the trash bin were, in the main, the historic doctrines of the Christian faith.

A primary component of this movement, and a radical departure from biblical orthodoxy, is the belief in the inherent goodness of man. Each human being is said to possess a divine spark. This theology admits to no demeaning "sinful nature" to degrade the nobility of man. The late Dr. Francis A. Schaeffer described the contrast:

> The Bible speaks to the man without the Bible—the man who is totally untrained in its content—and it speaks to the man with the Bible—the man who has had intimate exposure to its message. In both cases, it speaks to the fact that all men have sinned individually and as such are under moral guilt before God. This is a tremendous contrast to twentieth-century thinking in which man has guilt feelings but no true moral guilt, because there are no absolutes before which a

man is, or can be, morally guilty. Guilt feelings are all that are possible. But biblically all men stand guilty before God because each has deliberately sinned.[46]

To the liberal way of thinking, all that is necessary to fan the divine spark into a flame is the proper environment and a strong dose of do-goodism. While that flight of theological fantasy has long since been laid bare by the dreadful spiral of degeneracy we are experiencing, these wishful thinkers have not been dissuaded. Sadly, the "goodness of man" fiction permeates the thinking of all too many in the theological, psychological, and political realms as well as in the media. Typical of this new-age babble is the meandering of Dr. Wayne Dyer, a popular specialist in self-help psychology. Janet Parshall, in her book *The Light in the City*, comments,

> The reality of sin (and the need of a Savior) is absent from his psychospirituality. God is in everyone—and everyone is essentially divine. According to Dr. Dyer, all we have to do is tap into the divine nature that inhabits us all: There is not a separate God for each person. There is one universal intelligence flowing through all of us. That is the force of love. Remind yourself of that every time you doubt your own divinity. Affirm to yourself that you are divine and that you love and are loved and will not be pressured by your false-thinking ego to not know this. Remind yourself that the same force flows through you that flowed through Jesus Christ and Buddha.[47]

The ideology that framed such thinking and provided the basis for what we may term old-line ecumenicity ravished mainline churches, drove congregants out of the pews, and has proven a colossal failure. It is, for all practical purposes, passé. The new ecumenicity is an entirely different brand.

While retaining the concept of unity at the price of ortho-doxy, the new product is not confined to Protestant denomi-nations and related organizations. It is global in outlook, inclusivist to the core in nature, and espouses international unity with one notable exception: evangelicals, who refuse to march in lockstep with their newly enlightened "brethren."

In this new product, every religion, cult, and ism is accept-able, is equal in merit, and can serve whatever god is chosen, with full credibility ascribed to whatever practices seem proper.

In a real sense, the principle that levels industrial, social, and economic elements in secular global unity is reproduced in the world of religion. The reason for this is simple: Both systems are operating from philosophies gutted of spiritual absolutes, significant moral values, and respect for Judeo-Christian beliefs and founding principles. Therefore, those who don't agree are disenfranchised, subjected to ridicule, and stigmatized as obstacles to progress. In the secular venue, this would be mostly conservatives with strong nationalistic inclinations. In the realm of religion, this includes those who still cling to belief in the inerrancy of the Word of God and the conviction that the commission to evangelize is still an inescapable man-date—an obligation.

Come the Enforcers

Enforcement then comes to the fore as an issue to be dealt with. After all, if the world is being transformed into a truly unified global society—a global village, if you will, then signif-icant disagreement cannot be permitted. If the premise of the Dr. Dyers of the new world order is accepted—that "everyone is divine"—then those who attempt to convince people other-wise are disrupting the dignity of the gods and violating the rules of the game. Now the question becomes, What should be done with them? Enforcement usually begins with ridicule and repudiation, and then moves on to more stringent forms of action. The cold truth of the matter is that evangelical Christians are on a very precarious playing field, and like children walking against the light on a busy street at rush hour, many of us are completely oblivious to the danger.

Suffice it to say that the first salvos can be heard now. As we have seen in foregoing chapters, the mutilation of millions of Christians, multiple thousands of them Bible-believing evangelicals, goes on with hardly a whisper of opposition from ecumenical religious or secular communities. Above all, those who carry the gospel message bear a leprosy-like stigma that is deemed progressively more malignant and threatening in what is touted to be culturally elevated society. And like the lepers of ancient times, they are systematically segregated from the rest of society. Yes, we who are evangelical Christians are orphans in the global village.

Almost any way one chooses to look, the isolation of Christians from the mainstream is becoming more and more prevalent. Public education is a vivid example:

> Humanists and their bureaucratic allies are on an ideological search-and-destroy mission, determined to expunge even the mildest manifestations of religious values in public education. They have had notable successes: a graduating senior in New Orleans whose valedictory address was censored because she quoted the words of Christ; the child who was forbidden to read her Bible on a school bus; the third grader who couldn't display her valentines because they contained the inscription "I love Jesus."
>
> It has reached the point where public school students can experience anything...except God....It's only prayers, Bibles, and references to a supreme being which offend the sensibilities of secularist puritans.[48]

These are unquestionably overt acts of discrimination and persecution against Bible-believing Christians, their families, and the churches where they are taught to love Christ and have a proper reverence for the Word of God. This kind of persecution is intended to intimidate Christians, and, in unseemly ways, silence them.

What we've thus far failed to recognize is that these manifestations are only first-phase evidences of an escalating process of discrimination that will inevitably lead to even more harsh and restrictive attacks. Indeed, evangelicals are "orphans in the global village," and given the growing pressures to conform to ecumenical and secular expectations, remaining an evangelical Christian has the potential to bear extremely serious consequences.

CHAPTER SEVEN

I chose to stay motionless on the ground and hoped they would think I was already dead. A soldier came and shot my other leg. Then another came and fired two more bullets into my arm. I cried out to God in my heart, asking, "Lord, Lord, are you far from me?" He was not. God said to love your enemies as yourself. I thank God for protecting me; I am now nearer to Him.

JOHN KUOL
Sudan, 2002

When Cultures Collide

FOR THE LAST TWO CENTURIES, Christians in North America have enjoyed levels of religious freedom that are relatively unprecedanted for Christendom through the ages. The book *Unveiling Islam* paints well the grim picture that has been more the norm on this globe:

> For the other 95 percent of the world's population, conversion to Jesus Christ often means disowning, disinheritance, expulsion, arrest, and even death. In the world that does not embrace the "beliefs don't matter" mentality, the American attitude seems inane. At this moment, for the sake of the Gospel of Jesus Christ, men and women are being bullwhipped into submission, tortured, imprisoned, beaten, battered, and broken. Homes are being burned, families are executed, and other lives lost through hateful revenge. If you believe that torture and murder because of belief in Jesus Christ is a thing of the past, then you are tragically mistaken. Across our globe, the blood of Christians runs down cobblestone streets, dirt paths, paved alleys, and concrete prison floors.[49]

When Osama bin Laden orchestrated the catastrophic terror attacks on the twin towers of the World Trade Center and the Pentagon on September 11, 2001, there was an awakening of sorts. The arch-Islamist served notice on America and the West that a new wave of Muslim conquest had been launched in earnest. It had in fact been going on for years, but people at virtually every level of Western society failed to notice it—either deliberately or out of ignorance. Some voices attempted to raise warnings, but they became objects of ridicule and were written off as hysterical bigots who were not worth the time of day.

The depth of this calculated ignorance was highlighted when the distinguished *New York Times* Jewish journalist A. M. Rosenthal was awarded the Medal of Freedom in a White House ceremony on July 9, 2002. Five years before, Mr. Rosenthal had received a telephone call from another Jewish journalist, Michael Horowitz, telling the Pulitzer-Prize–winning writer that he was not doing his job: "Michael said that the biggest story in the world is the persecution of Christians. I found to my astonishment that it was true, said Mr. Rosenthal."[50]

For the next five years, Rosenthal wrote repeatedly about the persecution of religious minorities. In awarding the medal, President Bush honored the journalist for "his moral voice and mighty pen," which, "for decades, taught America and the world the folly and sin in the face of evil." The president noted further that Rosenthal was being honored for his "outspoken defense of persecuted Christians in Asia, Africa, and the Middle East [that] have truly made him his brother's keeper."

President Bush's words stunned journalists who accompanied Mr. Rosenthal to the White House—friends who were expecting the award to honor Mr. Rosenthal's decades of work at the *New York Times*. Their chin-dropping reaction is, says

Nina Shea, evidence that most journalists "move in a different world, Rosenthal stands alone within his world on this issue....The sad truth is that most journalists still tend to view Christians as persecutors, not persecutees, Ms. Shea adds."[51]

The significance of the "chin-dropping reaction" by the assembled journalists is that this award was presented nearly a full year after September 11. Dying Christians still do not matter. These same members of the journalistic elite have dedicated countless column inches to being apologists for Islam while ignoring any relationship between Muslim radicals, their commitment to *jihad,* and the religious holy war being waged against Christians the world over. Conversely, they consistently sell the idea that the Qur'an is a benign book and Islam is a peaceful, loving religion, which testifies to the fact that they have never seriously explored the content of the Qur'an or studied the often-bloody history of Islam.

The Trail of Blood

How can anyone—especially those in the media—ignore the horrific scenes being acted out on the world stage? Consider the following:

April 28, 2002—Black-clad Muslim warriors wielding swords and guns attacked Indonesian Christians in the village of Soya. At least 12 people were killed and six more injured during the attack. Thirty Christian homes and a Protestant church were burned down. The attack came only days after the Lasker Jihad leader called for Muslims to wage war on Christians.[52]

The Indonesian Lasker Jihad personifies the religious fanaticism that sees the slaughter of innocent Christians as a holy obligation. Stories of the heartless atrocities they revel in could fill a book. One such story has to do with Domingus Kenjam, a 20-year-old Bible school student who was awakened from sleep in his dormitory room by shouts of "Allah Ahkbar!" (God is great). Muslim attackers beat the young student mercilessly before he could attempt to flee. When he did try to leave, he was hit with a sickle. The blow nearly severed Domingus's head and he was left on the floor for dead. As medical personnel prepared to take him to the morgue, he said in a whisper, "I am a Christian." To everyone's surprise, Domingus survived. But he will wear the deep scars of the encounter for the remainder of his life.[53]

October 14, 2001—Muslim terrorists used the cover of anti-American riots being held to protest the bombing of bin Laden and the Taliban in Afghanistan to slaughter hundreds of Christians. In the city of Kano, those who survived death and injury fled to police stations and army barracks for safety. During their flight, dozens of churches were set on fire. Among those killed were six female secondary-school students who were on their way to take university exams.[54]

January 7, 2000—In Riyadh, Saudi Arabia, police broke up a Christian gathering of approximately 100 people and arrested 15 of them. Among those arrested were five children.

August 2002—In Jerusalem, on a day in late July, students, faculty, and employees were enjoying a leisurely lunch inside the popular Frank Sinatra Cafeteria on the campus of The Hebrew University. Without warning, a thunderous explosion ripped through the room. Terrorists from the Islamic Hamas organization had managed to infiltrate the restaurant and place a pipe bomb on one of the tables. When the smoke and dust cleared, seven people, five of them Americans, lay dead among the debris left by the explosion. At least 80 were counted among the wounded. A few days after the blast, two more victims died of wounds inflicted by the bomb.

Hamas claimed that they were striking back at Israelis for executing a high-ranking leader who was in the midst of planning a mega-terrorist attack inside Israel. The attack at the university, however, was not about killing only innocent Israeli civilians, who are targeted by terrorists as soldiers and therefore deemed legitimate prey for their guns and suicide bombs. The Hebrew University has for years had a reputation for moderation. In fact, of the 25,000 students enrolled, some 4,600 of them are Israeli Arabs. Approximately 1,900 are from abroad. All of which says that the objective of this monstrous attack was to kill anyone who happened to be at the wrong place at the wrong time.

Among the severely wounded at The Hebrew University were three devoted Christians from South Korea. You Kad Song, married and the father of a three-and-a-half-year-old boy, spent nearly two weeks in the intensive care unit of the Ein Kerem hospital. He was then moved to the plastic surgery wing for extensive repairs of his burns. Kuan Son Dal suffered extensive burns on his hands, legs, and face. Two weeks after the incident, he was still in a comalike state. Kuan is the father of a five-year-old boy and a little girl who is one. Zeng Se Ho also suffered serious burns on his face, hands, and legs. His condition was complicated by the fact that a table leg penetrated his body, necessitating the removal of three ribs. This married father of one daughter faces a long period of recovery.

In a display seen frequently in tragic circumstances, fellow Christians immediately came to the bedsides of the wounded men. While their wives kept a constant vigil at the hospital, the pastor of the church they attended in Jerusalem gave daily support for the families. In a moving display of Christian love, a choir of young people from the church came to sing for the injured men. Their mini-concert and the constant stream of concerned believers had a profound effect on the doctors and medical staff members caring for the men—so much so that a doctor took the pastor aside and questioned him about the faith of these Christians who demonstrated such a deep love for his patients. Once again, the biblical principle of the unifying force of suffering became a window through which people could witness firsthand the reality of faith triumphing over tragedy.

In the immediate aftermath of the bombing in Jerusalem, crowds of Palestinian Muslim radicals celebrated the attack by dancing in the streets and hailing the fact that Americans had been among the victims. Their festive display highlighted a manifestation that plagues the international community in this era in which, without question, a struggle of epic proportions is developing.

For example, in an article published in *National Review Online*—August 2, 2002—writer Bat Yeor lists grisly incidents confirming Islamists' indiscriminate slaughter of innocent people.

In Indonesia, some 200,000 deaths resulted from *jihad* violence in East Timor. Christians have been pursued and massacred, and their churches burned down by jihadists in the Moluccas and other Indonesian islands. The death toll in these violent attacks is more than 10,000, while an additional 8,000 Christians have been forcibly converted to Islam, including many who were circumcised.

Jihadists in the Philippines and some northern Nigerian states are also committing atrocities. Hundreds of innocent people died when *jihad* struck at the Jewish Community Center of Buenos Aires in Argentina and the U.S. embassies in Kenya and Tanzania. In Egypt, jihadists have massacred Copts in their churches and villages and murdered European tourists. Christians in Pakistan and in Iran live in terror of accusations of blasphemy, which, if proven, can yield a death sentence. And a cataclysmic act of *jihad* terror resulted in the slaughter of nearly 3,000 innocent civilians of multiple faiths and nationalities in New York, on September 11, 2001.

Cultures in Collision

September 11, 2001 clarified, in no uncertain terms, that there is a war going on. The conflict is not simply between radical Muslims and Israel and its Jewish citizenry, it is against Christians, democracy, and all that Judeo-Christian Western cultures represent. It is, in fact, a renewal of the Muslim wars of conquest that began under the prophet Muhammad during the sixth century.

As recently as the breakup of the Soviet Union and the end of the Cold War, wishful thinkers could not fathom the possibility of wars on the scale of what we are witnessing today. Intellectuals such as Francis Fukuyama expressed the delusional view that mankind was entering a humanist millennial new world order. "We may be witnessing," Fukuyama enthused, "the end of history as such: that is, the end point of mankind's ideological evolution and the universalization of Western liberal democracy as a final form of human government...the global conflict is over."[55]

Fukuyama and a host of others made the same potentially fatal mistake of believing that the age of global conflicts was over. Their rose-colored elitist optimism bore echoes of the World War I syndrome that Western democracies had fought and won "the war to end all wars." It took less than a generation to explode that myth.

When Samuel P. Huntington's *The Clash of Civilizations and the Remaking of World Order* was published in 1996, there were more than a few skeptics who questioned the validity of the book's message. Huntington's thesis expressed a central premise:

> The underlying problem for the West is not Islamic fundamentalism. It is Islam, a different civilization whose people are convinced of a superiority of their culture and are obsessed with the inferiority of their power. The problem for Islam is not the CIA or the U.S. Department of Defense. It is the West, a different civilization whose people are convinced of the universality of their culture and believe that their superiority, if declining power, imposes on them the obligation to extend that culture throughout the world. These are the basic ingredients that fuel the conflict between Islam and the West.[56]

Huntington states further, "Wherever one looks along the perimeter of Islam, Muslims have problems living peaceably with their neighbors." He then lists some revealing statistics, among them an analysis by Ruth Leger Sivard. She "identified 29 wars (defined as conflicts involving 1000 or more deaths in a year) underway in 1992. Nine of 12 intercivinizational conflicts were between Muslims and non-Muslims, and Muslims were once again fighting more wars than people in any other civilization."[57]

These words, written before September 11, 2001, were confirmed in one terrifying event. That horrific milestone, called by some the worst American tragedy in 100 years, exposed Osama bin Laden's al Qaeda, a sophisticated worldwide terrorist network fanatically dedicated to destroying Western democracy and its infidel people and establishing a global Islamic state.

The Bethlehem Model

The revered "little town of Bethlehem," the place of Jesus' birth, may serve as a microcosm of the struggle, one that magnifies the Islamists' determination to drive Christians out of the Islamic world. Before taking control of Bethlehem in December of 1995, Yasser Arafat made his intentions clear. On the occasion of his daughter's birth, he declared,

> The Israelis are mistaken if they think we do not have an alternative to negotiations. By Allah I swear they are wrong. The Palestinian people are prepared to sacrifice the last boy and the last girl so that the Palestinian flag will be flown over the walls, the churches, and the mosques of Jerusalem.[58]

At the official takeover in December of 1995, Christian pilgrims were greeted to a celebration of Muslim dominance over the town. A large image of Chairman Arafat's face covered several stories of a nearby building. Atop the Church of the Nativity in Manger Square, a platform had been constructed for Arafat's celebratory speech. Among other things he spoke of redeeming Jerusalem in spirit and in blood. One news headline declared, "A biblical city changes hands."

And the changes weren't long in coming. Arab Christians were subjected to what was described in a report from the Israeli prime minister's office as "relentless persecution." Christian cemeteries were desecrated; monasteries and convents have been broken into, and Christian community leaders and Palestinian converts to Christianity were intimidated. To make matters worse, many Arab Christian shop owners were forced to pay protection money to Palestinian thugs who were ignored by the Palestinian Authority.

As a result, many Christians whose families had lived in Bethlehem for multiple generations began to flee. Before the

Palestinian takeover, Bethlehem was 80 percent Christian Arab and 20 percent Muslim. As the exodus proceeded, the numbers were reversed. Christian Arabs numbered fewer than 20 percent, while Muslim population came to exceed 80 percent.

During the Al Aksa Intifada, Bethlehem was turned into a terrorist enclave from which suicide bombers and militants shot and harassed Israelis in the nearby suburbs of Jerusalem. At one point, approximately 100 terrorists took over the Church of the Nativity, and in the course of their standoff with Israeli Defense Force troops, they desecrated the sanctuary. When they finally vacated the premises, a heavy stench of urine and garbage permeated the church, which is situated immediately above the traditional place of Jesus' birth. It was, in fact, a rather symbolic manifestation of what is taking place in this epic clash of civilizations.

In mosques in many parts of the world, Muslim preachers deliver chilling diatribes against Jews, Americans, and Christian believers. Often they refer to Jewish people as the sons of "pigs" and "monkeys" and president Bush as another Hitler, and they pray for their destruction and that Allah will freeze the blood within their [Christians'] veins.

In France, where 6 million Muslims now live, there is an increasing level of tension that threatens to disrupt the government. Anti-Semitism is at the highest level there since the days of Adolph Hitler, and the radical Islamic hatred of Jewish people also extends to Christians.

On September 11, 2002, when most nations were solemnly commemorating the tragic attacks on America, Islamists in Great Britain, where there are now some 1000 mosques, held a celebration of the event at a conference in London. The leaders vowed to make England a Muslim state, establish Islamic law *(Shari'a)*, and attempt the overthrow of Prime Minister Tony Blair.

An Alarming Trend

What many in the West, Christians included, fail to understand is that Islam is not a pluralistic religion. It is exclusivist and it teaches that when the population of Muslims exceeds that of non-Muslims, then Islam should become the law of the land.

This is not to say that all Muslims are terrorists, and that there are not Islamic people who wish to live at peace with their neighbors. Many of these people will be quick to say that their religion has been highjacked by radicals who are giving their faith a bad name and thereby casting suspicion on all Muslims. This is true, and we must carefully guard against discrimination of innocent people on the basis of their religion.

Having said that, we must also acknowledge that radical forces in Islam are experiencing a rapid increase in the number of adherents who are fostering and perpetrating the slaughter of Christians at a rate unprecedented in our lifetime.

CHAPTER EIGHT

...be thou faithful unto death, and I will give thee a crown of life.

REVELATION 2:10

The Generation Gap?

IN RECENT YEARS WE HAVE HAD A PLETHORA of books, seminars, TV shows, academic and church discussion groups wrestling with the question of whether the generation gap exists, and how wide it is. No doubt there are formidable proponents in both camps. If you want to field test the issue, observe how most people over 60 respond when they walk into a trendy restaurant where they are immediately assaulted by a cacophony of ear-splitting noise and unintelligible howling that passes for contemporary musical artistry. It's an easy call. There is an impassable gulf between advocates and dissenters. Neither is inclined to give any quarter. However, other problems related to the innumerable issues dividing the generations are not confined to such trivial though irritating matters. In relation to the subject of Christian persecution, we must ask the question as to whether the gap exists, and if so, why?

The answer is a somewhat paradoxical yes and no. Yes, it does exist, but is it fundamentally different in the responses of both of the generations in question? The answer, unfortunately, is probably no or not much.

Shocking the Pollsters

An article in *The Washington Times* on August 31, 2002 raised eyebrows and more questions about what has afflicted us and where we are headed as we enter an uncertain and assuredly hostile global environment in the future:

> Britain's reputation as a land steeped in an appreciation of history has taken a hit with the publication of an opinion poll on what its masses consider the most important events of the past 100 years.
>
> The top of the list of momentous events in British history excluded both World Wars, the collapse of the British Empire and the rise of the Beatles to stardom.
>
> Instead, Britons said the death of Princess Diana— five years ago today—was the most significant event. This is a shocking result [said a historian and consultant to the UK History Channel].
>
> How Princess Diana's death gets rated the most significant event in British history in the past 100 years defeats me. But it shows how the impact of historical events is skewed toward more recent events where people's personal experiences come into play— and particularly if they are recorded as moving images....
>
> Age clearly affected the poll, as those with longer memories lent greater significance to more distant events. For instance, while 41 percent of all respondents said the September 11 terrorist attacks were the most important event in world history, only 28 percent of those older than 65 thought so....
>
> People look at history very much as it relates to their own lives, so more recent events will take on greater personal value.[59]

The most noteworthy observations regarding the poll results were that "the impact of historical events is skewed toward more recent events where people's personal experiences come into play" and "people look at history very much as it relates to their own lives."

Of course they do, and perhaps much of the inability of many in this generation to relate to past tragedies and apply the lessons to the future can be laid at the door of their forebears' failure to properly communicate what they witnessed during their lives.

Throughout the Old Testament of the Bible, there are reminders for the Jewish people to instruct their children in the history of their people, particularly as it related to communicating the commands of God. For example, Deuteronomy 6:6-7 says, "These words, which I command thee this day, shall be in thine heart. And thou shalt teach them diligently unto thy children, and shalt talk of them when thou sittest in thy house, and when thou walkest by the way, and when thou liest down, and when thou risest up."

I once had a Greek language instructor who began each class session by intoning the refrain, "The eternal price of knowledge is review, review, review." Although at the time I quickly became bored with his repetitious invocation, I am now well aware of what he was attempting to instill in his wards.

Walking Down Memory Lane

I made my inauspicious entry into this world in the spring of 1930. Although I wasn't aware of it at the time, America was in a tough spot. We didn't feel it as much as others because my father, employed in the aircraft industry, always had a job.

Others did not, however, and the early 1930s were a hard-scrabble time for most Americans.

But when I think back on my world, and compare it to the world of my grandchildren, the differences are of such magnitude that one can hardly begin to describe how it was in those days.

For instance, as a child I can remember the commemorations celebrated for those few withered Civil War veterans who were still alive. It was always a curiosity for me, as a boy, to hear the stories of the epic battles they had survived as drummers and standard bearers. Later, I learned of a relative who had been wounded in the terrible Battle of the Triangle at Spotsylvania Courthouse in Virginia.

One of my uncles had been a doughboy in World War I and could tell us of the mud, rats, mustard gas, and machine gun nests in the fields of France. He talked of terrible places such as the Argonne Forest and Belleau Wood. Our little town was the home to many who had marched away to fight the "war to end all wars." Many never made it back. As boys we would play on the memorial to the fallen, which stood on the main corner of town and listed the names of the dead heroes. The names were familiar to us all, and their families still lived up and down the washboard roads of our community.

On December 7, 1941, I was on my way home from the Sunday matinee at the downtown—such as it was—Civic Theater. I was stunned, but frankly relieved, to learn that we had entered the war against Germany and Japan. I remember sitting with father and the family, glued to the radio, as President Roosevelt solemnly declared war on those nations. As an 11-year-old, I heard over that same radio the charismatic voice of Adolph Hitler thundering his diatribes against Europe and the West. Although I couldn't understand a word, there was an inescapable dynamic in his demented voice.

The glamour ended quickly as the wounded began to come home. In a small town of about 2000 in Virginia, 23 young men were killed within the first few minutes of the D-Day assault at Normandy. Wounded survivors told grim tales of the horrors suffered at the hands of the Japanese or their stints as prisoners of war in internment camps in Germany. I remember the experience of the brother of a school chum who had been shot down while flying as a tail gunner in a B-17 bomber over Germany. Farmers tried to hack him to death with sickles before German soldiers could get to him and the other downed airmen.

In the newspaper, photographs of treeless vistas and the incinerated bodies of dead soldiers on islands in the Pacific were daily fare. Seeing the great cities like Munich turned into ashes during the massive bombing attacks over Germany and children and weeping mothers picking through the remains sobered even the hot-blooded advocates of unconditional surrender.

And then came the stunning revelations of the unspeakable horrors of the slaughter that took place in the German death camps. Some young American soldiers brought home snapshots they had taken in the camps. They showed us emaciated bodies stacked like cordwood or half-burned in the ovens of Auschwitz, Treblinka, and other death factories. General Eisenhower had sent them in on orders to look, remember, and take those memories back home. America must never forget, the future president firmly asserted.

After the war, we saw young men who came back as shells of what they had been. Many of them never recovered. They spent their nights in beer gardens trying to drink away the visions of what they had lived through. Others woke up screaming with nightmares of dead buddies and the horror of trying to stay alive. This is not melodramatic meandering; it was the stuff of real life for the people of my generation.

Remember that poll? We should know what it means. People are impacted most by the events that touch their own lives in personal and dramatic ways. I, and thousands of my contemporaries, can agree wholeheartedly. We carry a mental volume filled with memories. And in ways good and bad, we can never escape them.

An Environment of Certainties

It is not enough, however, to chronicle historical and social events of the past 70 or 80 years and assert that those monumental episodes will provide an adequate explanation of why there is a gulf between the generations. Nor is it profitable to hold these personal line-of-sight experiences up to our juniors as the test of whether they are worthy to stand with us on the holy ground of the past.

In the first place, the vast majority is not listening. Watch the expressions on the faces of the under-forties group in the family circle during holiday festivities when the "how tough it was for us" catalog is thrown open. Tales in the spirit of walking five miles to school in shoes riddled with holes in subzero weather and of snows that get deeper with every telling are greeted with rolling eyes, deep yawns, and "when can we leave?" looks.

It's all "ancient history." And to criticize younger people for the lack of interest in how it was for the older generation is actually quite unfair. To the younger generation, the life experiences of the older generation are ancient history. And, as it was with the older folks, they much prefer to be making history of their own.

To a great extent, the differences in the generation gap are in the diverse environments that shaped each generation. The

America of my generation was sure of itself. Ours was the best country in the world and we knew it. Though there were early warning signs that certain cultural tides were rising, they had not yet surfaced to the level where most Americans lived. We were certain that we were right in all our wars from World War I through the Korean conflict and that when the smoke cleared we would emerge victorious. There was never a question about it. No consensus as to whether these were "just wars" was ever sought, much less considered. Famous Civil War general Thomas J. (Stonewall) Jackson's military philosophy was still the order of the day: "I am a soldier," he said, "and a soldier's duty to his country is to fight."

There were absolutes to be served. Judeo-Christian mores dictated the cultural norms of the country. There was a basic unity in the philosophy of life in America. I suppose one could say that unity was the factor that reflected, in totality, what America was. Furthermore, the undergirding of that unity was the Bible.

For the following generation, however, the shape of the culture changed dramatically. The country was no longer self-assured and confident. Authority was being questioned, and there was a sociological revolution going on. Rebellion on college campuses was an unsettling reality. Vietnam tore the nation apart and instilled self-doubt, defeatism, and national humiliation. Veterans who had distinguished themselves in the service of their country were more often humiliated than honored. Politics took on an aura of being a dirty business. Corporations and big business were painted as near-criminal exploiters of the system.

Judge Bork spells it out when he addresses how television reflects the regressive elements in our culture:

> The moral relativism of the Sixties is now television's public morality. Though it cannot begin to match rap,

TV undermines authority in gentler ways. Families are relatively egalitarian; at work, subordinates ridicule their bosses and usually prevail over them. Businessmen are depicted negatively: they were three times more likely to commit crimes and five times as likely to be motivated by pure greed as people in most other occupations. Politicians fare no better. The military suffered a great fall in prestige beginning in the Sixties. Law enforcement officials are now shown as corrupt and as likely to commit crimes as anyone else, but criminals are portrayed sympathetically.[60]

The reason the medium of television is so important is because it is a line-of-sight industry. Thus, for millions, especially the young and those with little understanding of history, impressions and value judgments are drawn vicariously rather than experientially. The great pitfall here is that television is essentially an entertainment medium affected in life and death ways by the ratings system. Unfortunately, even the network news broadcasters are not above playing the ratings game.

Interestingly, the plot in a recent motion picture called for a Hollywood-produced "war" that would divert the country's attention from a president's indiscretions that threatened his reelection. When challenged by someone who thought the made-for-TV "war" a preposterous idea that no one would believe, the producer glibly replied: "Sure they'll believe it. Why? Because they saw it on TV."

His scripted answer expresses precisely what worries serious educators, who are faced with the same problem in the university classroom:

A professor of communications says that his students "tend to have an image-based standard of truth. If I ask, 'What evidence supports your view or contradicts it?'" they look at me as if I were from another planet.

It's very foreign to them to think in terms of truth,
logic, and evidence." Though this is a problem across
class lines, the situation becomes desperate for the
poorly educated....[61]

The disruption of reality-based thinking has encouraged
two elements to emerge in the American culture: uncertainty
and lack of trust in the American establishment, and a turning
to a more self-oriented lifestyle.

There has been, in fact, a not-so-subtle progression from
commitment to loyalties larger than self and self-interest to
being absorbed with a "me and mine" philosophy of life. This,
coupled with the scraping of biblical absolutes and values, has
introduced an era of doing one's best to extract from the system
everything that will contribute to one's personal wealth, welfare,
and fulfillment. In this not-so-brave new world, portfolios,
gadgets, and the glamour of living the good life are paramount
objectives. Among the most obvious manifestations of this
change is diminishing of the influence of churches, which are
being replaced by new houses of worship, such as sports sta-
diums and entertainment palaces. Like the ancient Romans,
more and more Americans are channeling their energies and
resources toward the spectacles offered by these arenas.

For some time now, the older and younger generations have
been operating on far different assumptions. They have been
living in separate worlds, and neither has yet grasped the
enormity of the differences. Conservative Christians, from
what may be termed traditional America, have held to the
belief that the old ways were still in play. But they were wrong.
Dr. Francis Schaeffer articulated this new fact of life some
three decades ago:

Whether we live in the United States, Britain, Canada,
Holland or other "Reformation countries," it really

does not matter. The historic Christian faith is in the minority. Most Christians, especially those of us who remember what the United States was like forty or fifty years ago, go on as if we were in the majority, as though the status quo belongs to us. It does not.[62]

He also commented with some trepidation about what he felt this would mean for the future.

The evangelical church seems to specialize in being behind [the times]...the major problem we are going to face—as I see it, and I could be wrong and I hope I am—in the next twenty five years or so is revolution with repression. Society is going to change. I believe that when my great-grandchildren grow to maturity, they will face a culture that has little similarity to ours. And the church today should be getting ready and talking about issues of tomorrow and not about issues of thirty or forty years ago, because the church is going to be squeezed in the wringer. If we have found it difficult in these last years, what are we going to do when we are faced with the real changes that are ahead?[63]

As Dr. Schaeffer lamented, the age of certainty, national self-confidence, and moral unity has been slipping into the sunset. And those of us who are older must guard against making the mistake of living in the past and in the process fail the generation we are charged to counsel wisely and biblically for the daunting future conflicts they will face. This is not a time for the wringing of hands and carping about the flaws we see in contemporary society and the church. There has been a cultural revolution in America with some very bad attributes, but the biblical injunctions to believers have not changed, and who better can we pass the torch to than those whom we have taken the time to help understand the issues.

Turning the Tide

We live in a secularized society and in secularized, sociological law. By sociological law we mean law that has no fixed base but law in which a group of people decides what is sociologically good for society at the given moment; and what they arbitrarily decide becomes law....Fredrick Moore Vinson (1890–1953), former Chief Justice of the United States Supreme Court, said, "Nothing is more certain in modern society than the principle that there are no absolutes." Those who hold this position themselves call it sociological law.[64]

Just what does this secularized, no absolutes society we now live in look like? As has been suggested, it is a society dominated by self, self-adoration, self-gratification, self-promotion, self-adornment, and self-determination. It is an environment that many, frankly, wonder if we can recover from. Judge Bork has some optimistic words on the dilemma; how can the tide be turned?

What may be feasible is a moral regeneration and an intellectual understanding capable of defeating modern liberalism. In a discussion of that possibility with friends, we came up with four events that could produce a moral and spiritual regeneration: a religious revival; the revival of public discourse about morality; a cataclysmic war; or an economic depression....

Perhaps the most promising development in our time is the rise of energetic, optimistic, and politically sophisticated religious conservatism. It may prove more powerful than merely political or economic conservatism because religious conservatism's objectives are cultural and moral as well....We may be witnessing a religious revival, another awakening....[65]

The judge's little group hit the proverbial nail on the head with their initial observation: *a religious revival.*

The concept of revival is, of course, not a new or novel thing. It is a turning back to the old ways. And while this may not seem palatable to some, it is an indispensable phenomenon found throughout the biblical record. The prophet Jeremiah said it well: "Thus saith the LORD, Stand in the ways, and see, and ask for the old paths, where is the good way, and walk in it, and ye shall find rest for your souls...(Jeremiah 6:16).

In every instance of biblical revival that comes to mind, two human forces were in play. First, there were the elderly saints who had experienced walking in the "old ways." They had experienced the certainties and firm footings of obeying the divine mandates. And second, there were the younger people. They were the next generation, if you will. And although many on both sides of the line might not have recognized how indispensable they were to one another, it was a fact.

How does it apply to us and the subject at hand? Well, if the younger generation has in many respects, as Charles Colson has reminded us, "been co-opted by the culture," we who are older can place a major portion of the responsibility at our own doorstep—that is, at the somewhat calloused feet of our generation. In a rather devastating sense, we have contributed to it by choosing withdrawal over engagement.

At the same time, however, it is equally clear that many in the younger generation have shunted aside their elders and disengaged from the spiritual heritage of their predecessors.

Both generations have walked the courses we've just described and done so at a terrible price—and this must be addressed and corrected.

CHAPTER NINE

Remember those who are in prison as if you were their fellow prisoners, and those who are mistreated as if you yourselves were suffering.

HEBREWS 13:3 (NIV)

But Why the Silence?

GRANTING THAT THE OLDER SET HAS BEEN exposed to more sobering aspects of life in America than their progeny, an extremely perplexing question arises. While the blood of the saints is wetting the earth on so many fronts the world over, why the deafening silence coming from both camps? It may seem strange to say, but for all of the finger pointing between the elders and their offspring on a variety of issues, there are none being leveled on the subject of who is failing our dying brethren. In a very real sense, when it comes to the persecution of Christians, no generation gap exists.

It would seem logical to assume that the generation that witnessed the horrors of the death camps in Europe firsthand or heard or read the stunning media reports of the Holocaust and other unspeakable atrocities would be expressing outrage and horror over the carnage wracking innumerable Christian communities. But such is not the case.

It was striking that during the first-anniversary commemoration of the September 11 tragedy, while a host of suffering people were remembered, there was no mention, not even in passing, of Christian martyrs. It was worthy of note that in

some commemorations, care was taken in public pronounce-
ments to name Muslims, Buddhists, Hindus, and other members of religious groups who had perished, but to my
knowledge, no mention was made of Christians. This may
have been expected in secular programs, but the same haunting
omissions were the case in Christian commemorations as well.
Churches by the hundreds across the land observed the day
with ceremonies honoring firemen, police, public officials, and
the victims' families. These commendable observances keyed
on patriotism and the memories of the heroes of that grimmest
of days. Unfortunately, Christian heroes and martyrs were
conspicuously missing from the litany. The omission can be
credited to simple oversight, and the sense that the two cases
differ in that they are unrelated. One may also conclude that so
far as our churches were concerned, there may have been
something symptomatic on display.

The "Feel Good" Church

None of us feel comfortable hearing this, but we are all, to
a greater or lesser degree, affected (or should we say afflicted?)
by the feel-goodism of the era. The theory of the power of
positive thinking—seeing good in everyone and everything—
which was once scorned as a variation of the inherent goodness
of man heresy, has become a staple in much of evangelical
thought and practice.

> It would be dishonest to claim that all, or even most,
> Christians in America have simply followed a [feel
> good] consumer gospel. A thoughtful Christianity still
> remains intact in the hearts of countless believers, as
> well as in many churches, schools, and homes. However,
> consumerism is widespread and increasingly combined
> with the shallower form of modern psychology. The

call to "seek peace and pursue it" has become, in many
churches, a ceaseless quest for personal tranquility: no
stress, no guilt, no "unhealthy" emotions. A prolihera-
tion of self-help and recovery groups feeds preoccupa-
tion with emotional well being.[66]

When pollster George Barna issued statistics predicting
that Yuppies were ready to begin returning to the church, there
was a flurry of comment and anticipation. Many baby boomers
had apparently tired of their toys, failed marriages, shattered
families, and the delusion that peace and fulfillment was to be
found in living life to the fullest in the here and now. Somehow
the "he who dies with the most toys wins" mantra was taking
on a hollow ring.

But their return to church left the establishment with a
dilemma. These people were the products of the 1960s. Thus
they were emerging from a hedonist mindset and lifestyle.
Judeo-Christian values and concepts, which had been so deni-
grated in the institutions they attended, were not available as a
fundamental foundation on which churches could expect to
build.

Church leaders were, therefore, faced with some new issues.
Yuppies would come into the Christian community with a
laundry list of their needs *as they conceived of them*. And the way
they conceived of those needs would not, in many cases, be
what could be termed traditional—that is, the need for personal
salvation, repentance, and a radical change of life and lifestyle.

The choice facing evangelicals was twofold: whether to
preach the gospel to the neophyte seekers as they entered
their midst then deal with their life needs through biblical
counsel, doctrinal instruction, and extended discipling, or
first respond to their needs as they perceived them and craft
programs accordingly. The rationale for this latter course
was that, while placing emphasis on entertainment centers,

self-help seminars, child-rearing clinics, seminars on how to repair broken families or those on how to manage stock port-folios, the gospel would somehow be applied through a process of osmosis. The question came down to this: At which end of the process would the gospel of God's grace be served? For many churches, the "bigger is better" option seemed best. Get the big numbers; the serious business of the mission could come later.

Admittedly, this scenario might seem an oversimplifica-tion. But in fact, the mood had already been set for a radical turn in this direction. Evangelicals were already in the process of being assimilated into the cultural mainstream. And the tendency toward entertainment and doctrinal superficiality was already well on the way to being an accepted part of reli-gious life. Author Paul Marshall comments on the trend:

> Evangelical media offer primarily a smorgasbord of entertainment stars and uniquely western self-improvement opportunities. In books, seminars, and TV shows, star motivational writers and speakers pro-vide steps for career achievement. Entertainers, televi-sion personalities, and Grammy Award-winning contemporary Christian music artists deliver tips for discovering inner peace and joy. Professional sports heroes and Olympic medallists contribute suggestions for accomplishing one's personal best. While worth-while things are said in these testimonials, profound human suffering is hardly ever mentioned.[67]

Over the past few decades, the vast overemphasis that the church has placed on relationships, family management, and interpersonal well-being has not served us well. To be sure, each of these areas is an important segment of Christian living. But some of us seem to have forgotten that each factor is only one segment of the whole. To make them everything isolates us from a host of larger issues that go unattended.

The Christian life is not all joy, happiness, and a feeling of well-being. And the arena in which we function in this world is not confined to me, my family circle, friends, and chosen associates; it is much, much more than this. If it is not, then life becomes a rather futile and fruitless endeavor.

I doubt very much that many in upscale evangelical congregations would "feel better" hearing about Yaqoob Masih, a 15-year-old Pakistani Christian who died after suffering excruciating torture at the hands of Pakistani police on June 27, 2002. Yaqoob was the only son of Anayat Masih, and had just started a job as a sweeper for the Customs Department of the government of Pakistan. What was the crime of this young Christian who was the sole support for his family? The boy's transgression was telling the truth when asked about a crime he had inadvertently overheard being planned by a corrupt public official. Because as a committed Christian he could not lie when pressed to do so, he was taken to a secluded place and severely tortured. Before being mercifully taken in death, his ribs were broken, his fingernails pulled out with pliers, and his body beaten beyond hope of recovery.

Nor would some of our friends find it pleasant to hear the story of 17-year-old Gulnaz. The girl lived with her family in an impoverished Christian enclave within the city of Faisalabad, Pakistan. Because she was from a poor family, the girl went to work as a telephone operator in order to raise money to send her 12-year-old brother to a Christian school. Because she was a Christian she was often insulted and pressured to embrace Islam. Gulnaz was told, "Beautiful girls like you should not remain in Christianity." Over a period of time, the pressure became so intense she felt compelled to leave her job. On June 14, 2002, a friend of the owner of the establishment approached the girl and began to fondle her body. When she resisted, he warned her that she would pay for not accepting his advances. He meant what he said. When Gulnaz returned to the office to collect her pay the next day, her attacker was waiting. Armed with a bottle of sulfuric acid, he assaulted her and threw the acid in her face. As she screamed with pain, he poured it over her breasts, arms, and legs. When she screamed for help and none came, he threw acid in her eyes, then forced her mouth open and emptied the bottle down the girl's throat. Because this 17-year-old protected her morals as a Christian, she is scarred for life.

These are not feel-good stories, and you can be sure that they won't be repeated from many evangelical pulpits or related in many Sunday school classes. Because, you see, 15-year-old Yaqoob was not a star player on some local American high school football team. And 17-year-old Gulnaz is not a cheer-leader or head of some student council. These kids live every day in a place where Christians pay for their faith, and some, as we have seen, with their lives. Among some haunting questions are these: Who is listening? Who is watching? Who even cares enough to inquire?

Our Silent and Weakened Pulpits

This is a subject that's very difficult for me to approach. I am, in my heart, a pastor. For over 24 years I labored in evangelical churches as an undershepherd of Jesus Christ. So even though the pastorate is not my current primary field of service, I am still a pastor. Furthermore, I am the friend of pastors. The difficulties they face today dwarf those encountered by me and my contemporaries 20 or 30 years ago.

But I am compelled to say that thousands of our pastors, televangelists, radio broadcasters, and church leaders are failing our people by remaining silent in the face of the unrelenting slaughter of our brothers and sisters in other parts of the world. It is ironic that while evangelicals are compassionate and giving people, there is virtually no action, concerted or individual, on this front. And it is difficult to buy into the idea that the fault lies completely with our corporate alliance with the secular culture status quo, although I do believe that is a major part of the problem.

Skimming the Surface

Several years ago, while conducting a conference in Pennsylvania, I was given a copy of a rural Amish newspaper. I was struck by a feature article that spoke of the Baptists' victory over the Amish in the quest for success in the world of religion.

"There can be no question," the writer said, "that the Baptists have taken the day. They have found an unbeatable secret of success that we can never hope to rival." And what was the Baptists' "secret of success"? It was "large parking lots and short sermons"!

As is so often the case in tongue-in-cheek satire, there is a cogent point being made. That cracker-barrel philosopher may have been ahead of his time, but he had caught the wind that was blowing toward the new age of upscale evangelical worship styles. Times have been changing, and not all the changes have been for the good.

Few will question that there is a not-so-quiet revolution taking place in the way we worship. Novelty and innovation have come to the fore in evangelical worship style. The problem is not with changes in the way some things are done, for change is always inevitable. The key is that the changes need to help enhance rather than degrade the worship experience.

I was speaking at a large church in California. The occasion was a Round Robin Prophecy Conference being sponsored by a number of prominent evangelical churches in the area. When I entered the auditorium, the pastor came up to me and asked if we could have a word.

"I hope you don't mind," he said, "but we have scheduled a concert to precede your sermon. We do this because we want to draw the young people."

"No," I replied, "I like good music; I'll enjoy it."

From a seat in the front pew, I eyed the "concert band" as they approached the platform. The musicians were dressed in white meat coats adorned with bottle caps and assorted other mini-advertisements stuck to their lapels. Following them was the "backup" team, several young ladies in garishly undersized garments.

The "concert" began with an earsplitting explosion of disharmony while the backup crew gyrated on risers behind the band. There were lyrics of a sort. But with the decibel level challenging the capacity of the ear canal, it was difficult to discern the message. Occasionally I thought I heard the word "Jesus" break out of the verbal storm, but couldn't make out what else was coming at me.

Knowing that this congregation was peppered with senior saints, I ventured a glance over my shoulder to see how they were bearing up. To my surprise, they were clapping along and rocking and rolling with the performers. I wondered fleetingly if I had lived too long.

When I stood to speak, it was immediately apparent to me that the congregation and the preacher were standing on separate planets. They had not been prepared for a prophetic sermon, and they had been exposed to a kind of entertainment that took them in the opposite direction. I labored with my topic for a full 15 minutes before the crowd settled down and began to hear what I had to say.

I realize this may seem an extreme situation. Some may feel this is a reactionary exercise by a not-so-with-it old guy. That may indeed play into the episode somewhat. But there is an issue at play here that begs to be addressed. It is a reflection of one of the distressing elements at work in the evangelical culture. That issue is a growing tendency toward superficial worship styles that are more attuned to entertainment than biblical and spiritual enlightenment.

The Amish wag was quite correct about our growing propensity for "short sermons." By that I mean that the primacy of the pulpit is being diminished. Pastors are too often "hired" as managers, counselors, and social directors rather than men of God burning with a passion to preach the Word. Indeed, church congregations tend to complain about serious Bible exposition and are seeking a more topical, how-to type of emphasis. Pastors are often urged to apply the principles espoused in popular seminar venues and do more consoling and counseling than preaching.

Diminishing the serious preaching of the Word of God in favor of choreographed superficiality is doing irreparable damage to the church of Jesus Christ. Nothing less than the faithful proclamation of God's Word will expose congregants to the manifold truths and ramifications of the Christian life— not the least of which is our obligation toward fellow saints, especially those suffering deprivation, persecution, and martyrdom.

Downgrading Prophetic Teaching

I was once approached at a prophecy conference by a pastor who seemed rather distressed. He explained that he didn't particularly appreciate many aspects of the prophetic teaching he was hearing.

"It's all so depressing," he said. "I want my people to hear happy things that will uplift them and make them feel better."

As a result of this sort of discomfort level, many pastors have diminished their prophetic preaching and teaching, or even given up on it. This is a serious omission. The proclamation of prophetic truth is an essential component in a well-balanced pulpit ministry. For starters, the Lord gave at least one-third of our Bible over to prophetic truth. That should be enough to tell us we need to give the subject a proper airing before the people in the pews of our churches, and there are dramatically important practical reasons why this is true.

Millions of grassroots Christians have developed a great hunger to understand what's going on today, where it's taking us, and what we should be doing about it. And these very concerns are the primary reason God gave us prophecies in the Bible.

There is an abundance of evidence to substantiate the desire of many believers to be taught how to understand our present day and the future. Just ask pastors, evangelists, Bible teachers, or broadcasters who consistently present sound and sane prophetic truth in their ministries. They will tell you that they are constantly overwhelmed by inquiries and besieged by people requesting more information about the end times.

And there is an odd irony about this phenomenon. Prophecy teachers of 100 years ago experienced this same demand for prophetic teaching in their day, too. Their ministries attracted multitudes of Christians who read their books, absorbed their teaching, and expected some aspect of prophetic discourse to be included in every protracted series of meetings.

For example, "an American milestone was reached with the 1878 publication of William E. Blackstone's book, *Jesus Is Coming*. The book instantly became a phenomenal success, and sales were soon being counted in the hundreds of thousands. The work, which is read as a classic today, has sold over a million copies and has been translated into 47 languages."[68]

There are ministers today who say that they have no personal position on the subject of Bible prophecy. To them, I suppose, it seems outmoded, unintellectual, too complicated to tackle, or has no relevance to their ministry. But in neglecting prophecy, they are neglecting a full one-third of God's message to His people, which is a sad commentary on the inadequacy of their ministries.

Prophetic teaching is vital for a number of reasons:

1. It provides indispensable perspective into what is taking place in contemporary culture in these last days. It brings us the ring of the prophet's voice with all of the commensurate warnings, admonitions, and pitfalls to avoid in navigating these trying times.

2. It provides a legitimate biblical background for associating current problems with biblical solutions. This is not doomsday theology. It is practical and necessary for a constructive Christian life. One lament of serious believers is the lack of contemporary application of God's truth that relates to some of the serious issues we face every day. Such application does not mean preaching from the front page of the newspaper, but rather, points out why these events may be occurring and how Christians should respond.

3. It provides a viable road map for future events that leads to a balanced attitude toward the world that is and how we fit into it. It also assures us that, while we

are not given every detail of what the future holds, there should be no surprises for a true believer.

4. Prophecy magnifies the sovereignty and majesty of God. In the frantic minds of millions or perhaps even billions of people, some Christians among them, the world is out of control and no one seems to be at the wheel. Prophecy illuminates in magnificent ways that there is a fully competent Captain in charge—that there is a symmetry and order to the events being lived out on the world stage, and that these events are all moving toward an orderly and objective consummation. The last chapter has already been written.

5. Prophecy trumpets the "blessed hope" (Titus 2:13) to the beleaguered, world-weary, and even self-absorbed Christian pilgrim. *Maranatha*, "Our Lord come," was the watchword of the early church. It is a word virtually lost to this generation. A few months ago, I was ministering in the Midwest. At the conclusion of the service, while departing worshipers greeted me and commented on my message, one lady approached, extended her hand, said only a single word, "Maranatha," and walked on. For me it was a breath of fresh air. Her matter-of-fact disposition expressed expectancy, confidence, and a degree of certainty.

A few days ago, a longtime friend and internationally known Christian broadcaster and I were talking on the phone after an interview. We were lamenting how little is heard today about the rapture, heaven, hell, and future events. Is it not true? Ask yourself how long it has been since you heard from the pulpit or on television sermons given over to the exposition of these topics. There are some notable exceptions, but, unfortunately, they are just that.

In Anticipation of Heaven

Among affluent Western believers, the longing for the imminent, at-any-moment return of Christ to call away His church may be a lost truth. But you can be assured that the loss is only regional. In countries where persecution mutilates and slaughters the saints, the anticipation of the blessed hope is a moment-by-moment heart cry. And while some theologians who specialize in tinkering with truth and complicating what God simplifies are trying to make a case that imminent doesn't mean imminent, it is a futile venture. That's what the promise of Christ's return meant to the early church. That's what it has meant to successive generations. And that is what the Scriptures plainly teach. The only reason these debunkers of imminence receive a hearing from many in this generation is that they really don't see the need. That is, they don't see it yet. Those who bleed for their faith do.

I have a near addiction to the old spirituals. Lyrics about golden slippers, chariots swinging down to carry us away, and walking those golden streets in the New Jerusalem do something to my heart that few things equal. They're all about heaven, glory, the Savior's face, and exchanging shabby cabins for glorious mansions in the sky.

I've often thought about why those simple, almost homely spirituals have such a magnetism about them. I do know why. And I think you probably do, too. They were sung by a people who were in the far country, longing for home. In other words, these people needed heaven. Many of us are, at the moment, not too sure about needing heaven, but eventually it will come

to that, and perhaps sooner than any of us suspect. You could
have said "Maranatha" to any of these people in the far country,
and the simple response would have been a firm "Amen" and
"Maranatha" in return.

May that become our response as well!

CHAPTER TEN

As he was come to the place of execution, and was taken from the hurdle, he fell down devoutly upon his knees, desiring Almighty God to forgive his enemies. Then stood he up and beheld the multitude, exhorting them in the most godly manner to follow the laws of God written in the Scriptures, and to beware of such teachers as they see contrary to Christ in their conversation and living. Then he was hanged up in the middle in chains of iron, and so consumed alive in the fire, praising the name of God so long as his life lasted....

LORD COBHAM
London, 1418

Where Are the Signs on the Churches?

IN HIS BOOK *THEIR BLOOD CRIES OUT,* author Paul Marshall shared this observation:

> Years ago, I drove up Bathurst Street on my way to work in Toronto. I would pass synagogues of varying strictness, but each had a sign for the passing cars, "Remember Soviet Jews." I did remember, since I was reminded every working day. Christians too need to be remembered. Where are the signs on the churches?[69]

Marshall asks a haunting question. Where, indeed, are the signs on the churches? The fact that there are no signs may to a great degree expose what's going on inside those sanctuaries. If there is lethargy, indifference, or just ignorance about the problem of Christian martyrs, things can and must be changed.

I cannot believe that true believers are coldly indifferent to the suffering of others. It is more, I think, a matter of a lack of information, or given such information, a feeling of helplessness and frustration about what to do. Inevitably, when I address the subject in public gatherings, people approach me with a personal question: "What can I do to help?" This says to me that evangelicals may be the sleeping giant when it comes to action on behalf of our suffering brethren, but that giant can be awakened.

Those synagogue signs that author Marshall saw every working day—"Remember Soviet Jews"—worked. Not that alleviating the persecution of Christians is as simple as posting signs outside buildings, but that they represent voices being heard. There is action being taken. In the end, not allowing politicians, community leaders, or human rights groups to forget the plight of Soviet Jewry was the driving force in opening the gates of freedom for imprisoned Soviet Jews. And one cannot help but consider it was an important element in the eventual demise of the U.S.S.R.

But what can we as Christians do?

Prayer, the First Priority

Believers have a resource not available to secular organizations: prayer. And prayer must become a priority rather than an add-on in any effort to help the persecuted. Intercession on behalf of fellow saints is high up on the scale of biblical imperatives.

During the fifth persecution of the early church, certain governing authorities were determined to destroy the church. To achieve the goal, Herod Agrippa decided to eliminate some of the church leaders. James, the brother of John, was executed, and the apostle Peter was incarcerated. Herod, no doubt, had the same destiny in mind for Peter as he had carried out for James. What did Peter's fellow believers do? Acts 12:5 tells us: "Peter, therefore, was kept in prison; but prayer was made without ceasing by the church unto God for him."

The consequence of this prayer vigil was the miraculous deliverance of the apostle. When he arrived at the gate of the house where the church members were engaged in prayer, they were astonished and couldn't believe he was a free man. God had heard and responded! Whether they fully realized the implications of concerted intercession or not, the Lord heard and answered. That message runs through the whole of Scripture and should resound continually in our ears.

It is most unfortunate that many of the prayer meetings conducted in evangelical churches have become halfhearted and superficial. Often the requests raised at these meetings have little to do with the truly heartfelt needs of the brethren, and even when they do, we seldom back up our prayers with the genuine passion and concern they deserve. Why don't we make a concerted effort to pray—as did Peter's companions—for the deliverance, safety, and intervention of God for suffering fellow believers outside the immediate circle of our church fellowship?

In order to pray efficiently and effectively, it is necessary for us to devote time and effort to learning the facts about what's happening to believers in other countries and cultures. Because Christian persecution is not something we see on the news channels nightly does not diminish the importance of our brethren's suffering. Don't expect the world to share your compassion and concern: Most people have neither the capacity nor desire to do so. And don't be deterred because of a lack of information from your church or denomination. Informing yourself may amount to launching a self-help program. The information is available; you'll just have to dig to get it.

Several years ago I was visiting a Jewish settlement, Kiryat Arba, near Hebron on the West Bank in Israel. The town has been attacked many times by those intent on killing Jewish settlers. In fact, the night before I came to interview the settlement director, an Orthodox religious Jewish man, a terrorist had come over the fence and tried to attack settlers. Among the questions I asked was why he and his family had chosen to live in such a dangerous place. He matter-of-factly told me that he felt they had no other choice; it was an obligation. When I responded that he was motivated by a sense of duty, he emphatically said, "No," explaining that there is a great deal of difference between duty and obligation.

"A duty," he said, "is something you, for whatever reason, feel committed to do. You may feel it is your duty to shave every morning. But that is not an obligation. An obligation compels you to do certain things. You have no choice in the matter, because it is an obligation. So, no matter how dangerous it becomes, we must stay. It is our obligation."

I was deeply touched by this man's devotion to a commitment he was certain was mandated by God. This is the spirit that should link Christians to suffering brethren no matter what their color or culture or the language impediments we may have in communicating with them. Remembering and reaching out in every way possible is not something we may or may not choose to do; it is an *obligation*.

We may not be in life-or-death situations in our communities, but they are in theirs, and we owe it to them to care enough to educate ourselves of their peril and seek ways to help.

In short, be informed. A bit later, I'll give suggestions about finding the information you need.

Become an Activist

Think of what a difference you can make by doing even simple things to make others aware of the persecution of Christians. Someone in one of those synagogues in Toronto came up with the idea of posting those "Remember Soviet

Jews" signs. Someone had those signs prepared and placed before the synagogues. And because some anonymous person acted, we are remembering those signs in this book.

Imagine for a moment, what would happen if every church in your town had a large sign out front with the words, "Remember Persecuted Christians." And what if our cars carried the same words on bumper stickers? I'm sure many people would begin asking us questions about persecuted Christians.

I'll give you an example from Israel. A few years ago an aged and revered rabbi from Brooklyn, New York, made an announcement that he was, at 91 years of age, planning to make his first pilgrimage to Israel. "And," he told his zealous followers, "when I arrive, the Messiah will arrive with me." The announcement electrified his disciples, who interpreted his statement to mean that he, Mendel Schneerson, was in fact himself the long-awaited deliverer. In Israel, banners, signs, bumper stickers, placards, and illuminated signs atop cars bore the words, "Prepare for the coming of the Messiah." As it turned out, the rabbi passed away before he could ever make the journey and passed off the scene as yet one more messianic pretender. However, those signs and emblems had virtually everyone in Israel talking about the coming of the Messiah and inquiring as to whether the end was near.

The impact of minority factions who advocate their cause aggressively is an extremely powerful force in our country today—so much so that it is almost as though we are a country dominated by vocal minorities. Among others, gays, feminists, radical environmentalists, and atheists are winning major concessions simply because they are willing to bellow their concepts of "rights" into the ears of susceptible politicians and local social revolutionaries.

At the voting booth, all of these factions combined are, in fact, miniscule. But they are extremely vocal, and politicians and people in the street are inclined to hear the loudest voices.

Consider the Hindus and their impact on the fast-food giant McDonalds. Animal-worshiping Hindus complained about eating, unaware, animal fats as they chomped their french fries, and filed a lawsuit. According to media reports, McDonalds paid over 10 million dollars to appease Hindus. I'm sure you're aware of other stories in which a small group of people were able to get a legal or political ruling in their favor in spite of the fact that they did not represent a majority of the populace.

The point is that certain groups, whether we agree with them or not, believe in their causes enough to make themselves heard loud and clear—to the point that action is taken to meet the demands of the group. And there is no reason why Christians cannot do more than complain and sit on the sidelines. National leaders will listen to you, too, but you must make yourself heard.

I'm not advocating going into the sign business or carrying placards outside fast-food establishments. What I am saying is that exposing people to the issues you are passionate about can be extremely effective. And those believers who do feel a God-given sense of obligation can inform themselves, take that information into their churches, Sunday school classes, and other functions and begin to make a real difference in getting the message out. That person could well be you.

Get Politically Involved

Many evangelical Christians shy away from any involvement in issues they feel are political. But no matter what your personal conviction on that score happens to be, the issue of

Christians being slaughtered is a cause you, as a believer, should be addressing before local and national political leaders. For Bible-believing Christians, this is a significant and legitimate issue. It is lamentable that the persecution of religious believers has become so prevalent in today's world.

Author Nina Shea shares this thought-provoking statement in her book *In the Lions' Den:*

> We know that the United States government has within its power and discretion the capacity to adopt policies that would be dramatically effective in curbing such religious reigns of terror and protecting the rights of all religious dissidents.[70]

Shea backs up her lamentation with biblical precedent. She draws from the book of Acts and the incident when the apostle Paul, on the basis of his Roman citizenship, demanded to be heard before Caesar.[71]

In late September of 2002, two bearded gunmen walked into the Karachi, Pakistan office of the Organization for Peace and Justice, a group that gives free legal advice to impoverished workers and women. They walked slowly through the office, identifying Christian employees by asking each worker to quote a familiar verse from the Qur'an. Eight Christians were located and separated from the rest of the workers. Showing no haste, six of the Christians were bound and gagged and tied to chairs side by side at a table in the library. Then, one by one, they were shot in the head at point-blank range. One man managed to flee into a bathroom, where he was pursued and killed. An eighth man was critically wounded with a gunshot to the head.

"I would rate this as the most tragic terrorist incident since 9/11," said the local police chief. "Unlike the usual terrorists, the killers showed no haste. They took a good 15 minutes in segregating the Christians and making sure that each one of their targets gets the most horrific death."[72]

There can be no doubt that Christians in Pakistan are marked for execution. A Karachi police official said, "We have found a bunch of charts and handmade maps on Christian targets from their hide-outs."[73]

The reason given for the murders was radical Islamic anger against Pakistani president, Pervez Musharraf, for supporting the United States in the war against the al Qaeda and the Taliban. Although the rationale for the killings was clearly a ruse, Christians are frequently slain in Pakistan, and this is a matter that directly involves the United States. Therefore, our government has an obligation to respond and demand that such atrocities be stopped.

If, as Nina Shea points out, the U.S. government has been indifferent to its obligation to speak out against acts of terror now being plotted and waged against Christians, then Christians cannot be silent. To do so is a gross violation of our responsibility to speak on behalf of those brethren who have been silenced by bullets through their heads.

Some steps that can be taken by the government were provided in the Statement of Conscience issued by the National Association of Evangelicals and widely endorsed by national leaders, religious groups, and human rights agencies:

- There must be public acknowledgement of widespread and mounting anti-Christian persecution in the world and a public commitment by the president to public diplomacy openly condemning such persecution.

- The president should appoint a knowledgable, experienced, and compassionate special advisor to the president for religious liberty to prepare a report outlining the policy changes that are needed.

- The United States delegate to the United Nations Commission on Human Rights needs to raise this issue regularly and forcefully.

- Ambassadors and other diplomatic officials need to meet regularly with willing church leaders and dissidents.

- The State Department's human rights reports need to add a specific focus on such persecution, and reporting officers should be equipped to be able to distinguish the different types of groups affected.

- We should terminate our assistance to foreign countries that do not take action to end persecution.

These are among actions that are well within the province of the president and the governing officials of the United States. What is needed most now is a unified chorus of concerned citizens who articulate the need for action.

Dr Schaeffer spoke to the point:

> We do not need 51 percent of the people to begin to have an influence. If 20 percent of the American population were really regenerate Christians, clear about their doctrines, beliefs and values, taking truth seriously, taking a consistent position, we could begin, not to have an overwhelming consensus, but at least to have a vital voice again in the midst of our community. But if this reformation and revival, this positive revolution, does not take place, if we do not begin to put a positive base back under our culture, the base that was there in the first place and now is completely gone, then I believe with all my heart that we will have a revolution from either the left or the establishment in order to give at least an illusion of what the people want concerning

material well-being....And if this revolution comes
from either side, our culture will be changed still *further*. The last remnants of Christian memory in the
culture will be eliminated, and freedoms will be gone.[74]

There are many issues related to Christian activism and
political participation that we may choose to debate. This is
one issue, however, that is not debatable. Brothers, sisters, and
innocent children are bleeding, dying, and crying for someone
to help. If we choose to ignore them, for whatever reason, we
will, in the end, answer to our God.

Be There to Help

When those six innocent Christian aid workers in Pakistan were gagged, tied to chairs, blindfolded, and summarily
shot through their heads, no one was there to help. When a
boy with a nearly severed head needed assistance, no one was
there to help. When a young girl screamed for someone to
come to her aid as acid was being poured over her body, no one
was there to help. When black Sudanese children cried out in
agony as they were torn from their parents' arms, raped, bru-
talized, and sold into slavery, no one was there to help. We
cannot live with this any longer. We *must* be there.

Let's begin to be signmakers, and let's decide to be torch-
bearers for those who cannot help themselves. Remember...
what's displayed out front is often a vivid revelation to others of
the heart that's inside the person willing to reach out.

HELPING THE PERSECUTED

To get the latest updates on the persecution of Christians worldwide and find out how you can pray and help, contact the ministries listed below and check their web sites.

International Christian Concern
2020 Pennsylvania Avenue NW, #941
Washington, D.C. 20006
(301) 989-1708
www.persecution.org

Worthy Persecution News
www.worthynews.com/christian-persecution/

American Anti-Slavery Group
198 Tremont Street #421
Boston, MA 02116
(617) 426-8161
www.iabolish.com

The Voice of the Martyrs
P.O. Box 443
Bartlesville, OK 74005
(918) 337-8015
www.persecution.com

Samaritan's Purse
P.O. Box 3000
Boone, NC 28607
(828) 262-1980
www.samaritanspurse.org

National Association of Evangelicals
P.O. Box 28
Wheaton, IL 60189
(630) 665-0500
www.nae.net

Bibliography

Bennett, William J. *The Index of Leading Cultural Indicators: American Society at the End of the Twentieth Century.* New York: Broadway Books, 1999.

Berry, Grinton W. (ed.). *Foxe's Book of Martyrs.* Grand Rapids, MI: Baker Book House, 1997.

Bork, Robert H. *Slouching Towards Gomorrah.* New York: Regan Books, 1996.

Caner, Irgun M. and Emir F. *Unveiling Islam.* Grand Rapids, MI: Kregel Publications, 2002.

Elliot, Elisabeth. *Through Gates of Splendor.* Wheaton, IL: Tyndale House, 1981.

————. *Shadow of the Almighty.* San Francisco: Harper Collins, 1979.

Feder, Don. *A Jewish Conservative Looks at Pagan America.* Lafayette, LA: Huntington House, 1993.

Hitchens, Peter. *The Abolition of Britain.* San Francisco: Encounter Books, 2000.

Huntington, Samuel P. *The Clash of Civilizations and the Remaking of World Order.* New York: Touchstone, 1997.

Marshall, Paul. *Their Blood Cries Out.* Dallas, TX: Word Publishing, 1997.

McQuaid, Elwood. *The Zion Connection.* Eugene, OR: Harvest House Publishers, 1996.

Parshall, Janet and Craig. *The Light in the City.* Nashville, TN: Thomas Nelson Publishers, 2000.

Prager, Dennis. *Think a Second Time.* New York: HarperCollins, 1995.

Schaeffer, Francis A. *A Christian Manifesto*. Wheaton, IL: Crossway Books, 1982.

————. *The Church at the End of the 20ᵗʰ Century*. Wheaton, IL: Crossway Books, 1994.

Shea, Nina. *In the Lions' Den*. Nashville, TN: Broadman & Holman Publishers, 1997.

Staines, Gladys J. *Burnt Alive*. Mumbai, India: GLS Publishing, 1999.

Notes

1. Art Buchwald, "To Lose One's Center," *Jewish World Review* (September 10, 2002).

2. William J. Bennett, *The Index of Leading Cultural Indicators—American Society at the End of the Twentieth Century* (New York: Broadway Books, 1999) p. 5.

3. Gladys J. Staines, *Burnt Alive* (Mumbai, India: GLS Publishing 1999), pp. 15-16, 35-36.

4. Staines, *Burnt Alive*, p. 51.

5. Elisabeth Elliot, *Shadow of the Almighty* (San Francisco: Harper, 1958), p. 15.

6. Bennett, *The Index of Leading Cultural Indicators*, (New York: Broadway Books, 1999) pp. 4-5.

7. Bennett, *The Index of Leading Cultural Indicators*, pp. 176, 174.

8. Robert H. Bork, *Slouching Towards Gomorrah* (New York: Regan Books, 1997), p. 272.

9. Peter Hitchens, "The Abolition of Britain from Winston Churchill to Princess Diana," a review in *Wall Street Journal Europe.*

10. Peter Hitchens, *The Abolition of Britain from Winston Churchill to Princess Diana* (San Francisco: Encounter Books, 2000), p. 76.

11. Ibid., pp. 200-201.

12. Ibid., pp. 23-24.

13. Ibid., p. 105.

14. Ibid., p. 108.

15. Ibid., p. 176.

16. Ibid., p. 71.

17. Ibid., p. 73.

18. Ibid., p. 136.

19. David Klinghoffer, "Trendy Sermons, Vacant Pews," *Wall Street Journal* (January 3, 1997).

20. Bork, *Slouching Towards Gomorrah*, p. 281.

21. Ibid., pp. 279-280.

22. William J. Bennett, *The Index of Leading Cultural Indicators*, p. 174.

23. Bork, *Slouching Towards Gomorrah*, p. 281.

24. Ibid., p. 274.

25. Ibid., p. 278.

26. Klinghoffer, "Trendy Sermons, Vacant Pews."

27. Dennis Prager, *Think a Second Time* (New York: Regan Books, 1995), p. 5.

28. Gene Edward Veith, "Christians as Taliban," *World* (January 19, 2002), p. 14.

29. Bork, *Slouching Towards Gomorrah*, p. 291.

30. Ibid., p. 290.

31. Don Feder, *A Jewish Conservative Looks at Pagan America* (Lafayette, LA: Huntington House Publishers, 1993), p. 149.

32. Paul Marshall with Lela Gilbert, *Their Blood Cries Out* (Dallas, TX: Word Publishing, 1977), p. 163.

33. Bork, *Slouching Towards Gomorrah*, p. 294.

34. Prager, *Think a Second Time*, p. 78.

35. Joyce Howard Price, "Princeton bioethicist argues Christianity hurts animals," *The Washington Times*, July 4, 2002.

36. Paul Johnson, *A History of Christianity* (New York, Simon and Schuster, 1976), p. 517.

37. Nina Shea, *In the Lions' Den* (Nashville, TN: Broadman & Holman Publishers, 1997), p. 32.

38. Marshall, *Their Blood Cries Out,* pp. 150-151.

39. Revelation 3:17.

40. Marshall, *Their Blood Cries Out,* pp. 151-152.

41. Ibid., p. 63.

42. Staines, *Burnt Alive,* p. 165.

43. Francis A. Schaeffer, *The Church at the End of the 20th Century* (Wheaton, IL: Crossway Books, 1994), p. 5.

44. Janet and Craig Parshall, *The Light in the City* (Nashville, TN: Thomas Nelson Publishers, 2000), p. xvii.

45. Parshall, *The Light in the City,* p. xvii.

46. Schaeffer, *The Church at the End of the 20th Century,* pp. 48-49.

47. Parshall, *The Light in the City,* p. 21.

48. Feder, *A Jewish Conservative Looks at Pagan America,* pp. 50-51.

49. Ergun M. and Emir F. Caner, *Unveiling Islam: An Insider's Look at Muslim Life and Beliefs* (Grand Rapids, MI: Kregel Publications, 2002), pp. 15-16.

50. *World* (July 20, 2002), p. 5.

51. Ibid.

52. Goodenough, "Christians Killed in Renewed Attacks in Indonesia," CNSNEWS.com, April 29, 2002.

53. "I know the Plans I Have for You," Steve Cleary with Gary Lane, *Voice of the Martyrs* (May 2002), p. 3.

54. "Riots in Kano, Nigeria, International Christian Concern," www.persecution.org. October 14, 2001.

55. Samuel P. Huntington, *The Clash of Civilizations and the Remaking of World Order* (New York: Touchstone Books, 1996), p. 31.

56. Ibid., 217-218.

57. Ibid., pp. 256-257.

58. Speech given by Yasser Arafat on August 6, 1995, *The Jerusalem Post* (September 7, 1995).

59. Peter Almond, UPI, *Washington Times,* "Rue Britannia: Diana's death tops poll" (August 31, 2002).

60. Bork, *Slouching Towards Gomorrah,* p. 127.

61. Ibid., p. 253.

62. Schaeffer, *The Church at the End of the 20th Century,* p. 78.

63. Ibid., p. 77.

64. Francis A. Schaeffer, *A Christian Manifesto* (Wheaton, IL: Crossway Books, 1981), p. 41.

65. Bork, *Slouching Towards Gomorrah,* p. 336.

66. Marshall, *Their Blood Cries Out,* p. 153.

67. Ibid., p. 153.

68. Elwood McQuaid, *The Zion Connection* (Eugene, OR: Harvest House Publishers, 1996), p. 109.

69. Marshall, *Their Blood Cries Out,* p. 222.

70. Shea, *In the Lions' Den,* p. 98.

71. Ibid., p. 93.

72. Kamran Khan, "Seven Christians Executed at Charity in Pakistan," *The Washington Post* (September 25, 2002).

73. Ibid.

74. Schaeffer, *The Church at the End of the 20th Century,* p. 43.

Other Good Harvest House Reading

The God You Can Trust
Ray Pritchard

It's one thing to trust God when all is going well. It's something else to trust Him when life is falling apart. But God is faithful and promises to care for us. Discover the hope that comes from placing all your concerns in God's hands.

Unholy War
Randall Price

Why does strife continue in the Middle East? How is it connected to terrorist attacks on Western nations? Dr. Price provides a concise, fascinating look at the problems and the players in the Middle East.

In the Name of God
Timothy J. Demy & Gary P. Stewart

The shocking events of September 11 awakened Americans to the reality of faith-based terrorism. In this authoritative book, experts Demy and Stewart examine the connection between religion and terrorism and explore how Christians can respond.